CONTENTS

ACKNOWLEDGEMENTS

The Centre for Effective Services (CES) would like to acknowledge the help and support of all those who participated in the development of this report, particularly those who participated in the survey or agreed to be interviewed, and whose commitment to improving the lives of the children they worked with or on behalf of came across very strongly.

Particular thanks also go to the following for their help and expertise in shaping the report:

- Michele Clarke, Fergal Conlan, Noreen Leahy and Liz Canavan of the Department of Children and Youth Affairs;
- Dr. Paula Mayock, Assistant Professor, School of Social Work and Social Policy, and Senior Researcher, Children's Research Centre, Trinity College, Dublin;
- Terry Brophy, Service Manager, St. Catherine's Foyer;
- Eilis O'Connor, Crisis Intervention Centre, Health Service Executive (HSE);
- Siobhán Mugan, National Specialist, Alternative Care, Children and Family Services, HSE;
- Karen McAuley, Participation and Education Officer, Ombudsman for Children's Office.

EVERY CHILD A HOME

A REVIEW OF THE IMPLEMENTATION OF THE YOUTH HOMELESSNESS STRATEGY

2013
DEPARTMENT OF CHILDREN AND YOUTH AFFAIRS

The authors of this report are:
Sean Denyer, **Aisling Sheehan** and **Avery Bowser** of the Centre for Effective Services.

Department of Children and Youth Affairs
43-49 Mespil Road
Dublin 4
Tel: +353 (0)1 647 3000
Fax: +353 (0)1 667 0826
E-mail: contact@dcya.gov.ie
Web: www.dcya.ie

Published by Government Publications, Dublin

ISBN 978-1-4064-2771-4

The views expressed in this report are those of the authors and not necessarily those of the Department of Children and Youth Affairs.

An Roinn Leanaí agus Gnóthaí Óige
Department of Children and Youth Affairs

CES CENTRE FOR EFFECTIVE SERVICES

ACRONYMS

CAMHS	Child and Adolescent Mental Health Services
CIS	Crisis Intervention Service
DCYA	Department of Children and Youth Affairs
DSP	Department of Social Protection
EPIC	Empowering Young People in Care
ERHA	Eastern Regional Health Authority
ETHOS	European Typology of Homelessness and Housing Exclusion
FEANTSA	Fédération Européenne d'Associations Nationales Travaillant avec les Sans-Abri (European Federation of National Associations Working with the Homeless)
HIQA	Health Information and Quality Authority
HSE	Health Service Executive
LGBT	Lesbian, Gay, Bisexual and Transgender
MHB	Midlands Health Board
MWHB	Mid-Western Health Board
NCO	National Children's Office
NEHB	North Eastern Health Board
NEPS	National Educational Psychological Service
NEWB	National Educational Welfare Board
NWHB	North Western Health Board
OMCYA	Office of the Minister for Children and Youth Affairs
PASS	Pathway Accommodation and Support System
SEHB	South Eastern Health Board
SHB	Southern Health Board
WHB	Western Health Board
YHSMC	Youth Homelessness Strategy Monitoring Committee

GLOSSARY

Aftercare

Aftercare is the provision of services for children and young people who are leaving the care system at 18 years of age. Aftercare services are provided up until the maximum of 23 years of age and include the provision of advice, support and accommodation.

Care Order

The Health Service Executive (HSE) may apply to the Courts for a number of different care orders, which place the child in the care of the HSE either temporarily or permanently, with the exception of a Supervision Order.

Child and Family Agency

The Child and Family Agency is a new agency due to be established in 2013, which will assume full statutory responsibility for services for children, young people and families.

Children's Services Committees

Children's Services Committees provide a structure to bring together a diverse group of agencies in local county areas to engage in joint planning and interagency collaboration in the delivery of services for children and young people. Four Children's Services Committees were established in 2007 and the aim is that 20 or more will be in operation by the end of 2012.

Community development

Community development is about enabling people to enhance their capacity to play a role in the society of which they are a part. It works towards helping groups and communities to articulate needs and viewpoints and to take part in collective action to influence the processes that structure their everyday lives. The priority for those engaged in integrated local development is to work with the most disadvantaged.

Early intervention

Early intervention means intervening at a young age or early on in a problem. Early intervention helps those at risk to realise their potential and can support them and their families to become healthier and more resilient.

High Support Units

High Support Units offer a residential service to children and young people who are in need of specialised targeted intervention: they are 'open', in that the child is not detained. High support differs from ordinary residential care in that the Units offer higher staff ratios and on-site education, as well as specialised input such as psychology services. They aim to assist young people in developing internal controls of behaviour, to enhance self-esteem, facilitate personal abilities and strengths, and to build a capacity for constructive choice, resilience and responsibility. There are 2 national High Support Units under the governance of the National High Support and Special Care Service (Rath na nÓg, Castleblaney, and Crannóg Nua, Portrane), with a total of 11 places.

Housing First

'Housing First' is an alternative to the current system of providing emergency shelter/ transitional housing before obtaining independent housing, which tends to prolong the length of homelessness. People are instead moved immediately into their own independent accommodation. The thinking behind this approach is that vulnerable and at-risk people are more responsive to interventions and social services support after they are in their own housing, where they can regain self-confidence and control over their lives.

Implementation

Implementation can be described as the carrying out of a plan, a method or any design for doing something. It is about the 'how', rather than the 'what'. Implementation has also been defined as a set of deliberate and sequential activities designed to put a definite policy, plan or procedure into effect.

Local development

Local development is the development of area-based interventions to complement mainstream or structural policies addressing long-term unemployment, economic marginalisation and social exclusion. The aim of local development is to provide the structure, funding and support for the statutory sector, community sector and traditional social partners to act together for the benefit of the area.

Prevention

Prevention is stopping a problem from arising or preventing a situation from getting worse.

Section 5

Section 5 of the Child Care Act 1991 states: 'Where it appears that a child in its area is homeless, the health board shall enquire into the child's circumstances, and if the board is satisfied that there is no accommodation available to him which he can reasonably occupy, then, unless the child is received into the care of the board under the provision of this Act, the board shall take such steps as are reasonable to make available suitable accommodation for him.'

Special Care Units

Special care involves the detention of a child for his or her own welfare and protection in a Special Care Unit with on-site educational and therapeutic supports. The detention, by order of the High Court, is considered as a last resort, for as short a time as possible and when other forms of residential or community care are considered to be unsuitable. There are 3 designated Special Care Units in the country, operated by the HSE under a single national governance arrangement. They are Ballydowd Young People's Centre (Dublin), Glean Alainn (Cork) and Coovagh House (Limerick).

Supported lodgings

Supported lodgings is the term used for the provision of accommodation, support and in a domestic setting to young people who cannot live at home, but are not ready to live independently. The provider of supported lodgings will work in partnership with the young person and the young person's social worker in preparing them for independent living at a future date.

Voluntary care

The HSE may provide care for children and young people who can no longer be cared for by their family in their own home. Where parents agree to their children being taken into the care of the HSE, it is known as voluntary care. The HSE is obliged to maintain these children and young people for as long as their welfare requires it.

Youth work

A planned programme of education designed for the purpose of aiding and enhancing the personal and social development of young people through their voluntary involvement, and which is complementary to their formal, academic or vocational education and training and provided primarily by voluntary youth work organisations.

EXECUTIVE SUMMARY

Purpose of the report

This report presents the findings of a high-level review of the implementation of the Youth Homelessness Strategy. The purpose of the review is to establish the extent to which the strategy has been successful, to identify blockages and challenges to its implementation, and to make recommendations on a new implementation framework.

Background to the Youth Homelessness Strategy

The Youth Homelessness Strategy for children under 18 years of age was published in 2001 and its goal is:

> 'to reduce and if possible eliminate youth homelessness through preventative strategies and where a child becomes homeless to ensure that he/she benefits from a comprehensive range of services aimed at re-integrating him/her into his/her community as quickly as possible'.

The 12 objectives of the strategy (*see Appendix A*) fall under one of three categories, namely: preventive measures, responsive services, and planning and administrative supports. The definition of youth homelessness in the strategy is:

> 'Those who are sleeping on the streets or in other places not intended for night-time accommodation or not providing safe protection from the elements or those whose usual night-time residence is a public or private shelter, emergency lodging, B&B or such, providing protection from the elements but lacking the other characteristics of a home and/or intended only for a short stay.'

Included within this meaning are 'young people who look for accommodation from the Eastern Health Board Out-of-Hours Service and those in insecure accommodation with relatives or friends regarded as inappropriate, that is to say where the young person is placed at risk or where he or she is not in a position to remain'.

Methodology

The review consisted of the examination of key documentation; in-depth semi-structured interviews with a selection of stakeholders and service users; a web-based survey; analysis of key data provided by the HSE on service utilisation; and a workshop with stakeholders to validate the synthesis of findings in relation to each objective of the strategy.

Some significant changes occurred in the range of accommodation available to the youth homeless services during the course of writing this report and in some instances valid criticisms by stakeholders had been addressed or were being reviewed by the time this review was concluded.

Consultation with stakeholders: A consensus view

There was a great degree of consensus among stakeholders in relation to what they would like to see in the future:

- **A comprehensive and integrated multi-agency approach** to meeting the needs of vulnerable or at-risk children, which recognises the factors contributing to children and young people being out-of-home and at risk of homelessness, and addresses them with timely, effective and acceptable service responses.
- An emphasis on **prevention and early intervention**, which facilitates an early exit from homelessness where it does occur.
- **Flexible responses** in terms of accommodation and a flexible approach by services to meeting local needs.
- A **planned and coherent transition into productive adulthood** for children and a managed transition into adult services if required.
- That those young people over 18 years of age known to be particularly vulnerable to homelessness, because of having a history of being in residential or short-term foster care, receive **high-quality aftercare support.**
- **Information and decision support systems** that enable policy-makers, service planners and providers to monitor and evaluate activity, examine trends and adapt practice and policy accordingly.
- **A change of descriptor from 'homelessness' to 'out-of-home'**, which more accurately reflects the range of situations children may be in, so that in future we refer to children and young people as being out-of-home or at risk of being out-of-home.

Overall conclusion

It is clear from this review that homelessness for children under 18 years of age is rarely an isolated need and that the pathways into homelessness are complex. Outcomes for children who are out-of-home have improved over the last decade. More children are dealt with by way of preventive services or, if out-of-home, by better care services. To ensure this trend of prevention or early exit from homelessness continues requires a holistic view of the lives of children. There is no room for complacency and improvements are needed in providing children at risk with responses based on a comprehensive assessment of need and the provision of high-quality services and accommodation options to meet those needs. Key to improving outcomes for children is ensuring their transition to adult services is appropriate to their needs.

What is needed now is *not* another strategy for youth homelessness, but for the problem of children being out-of-home or at risk of homelessness to be addressed as part of a wider, integrated and 'whole child' response to need.

Key findings from the review

- Overall, the Youth Homelessness Strategy was felt to have made a significant contribution to addressing the problem of youth homelessness, as it was defined in the strategy, and at the extreme end has helped ensure that children sleeping rough on the streets is very rare. **The number of children who are homeless or at risk of homelessness has diminished** over the course of the strategy.
- There was widespread agreement among stakeholders that the strategy had successfully facilitated **considerable improvements in accommodation options and services** to support children experiencing, or at risk of experiencing, homelessness.
- **Investment in child protection and welfare services, fostering, family support and youth services** appear to have made a positive impact on the experience of children presenting as homeless or at risk of homelessness.
- Children who present to services as homeless or at risk of homelessness are now generally **assessed and provided with services** on the same basis as children who present with protection and welfare concerns.
- The review of the effectiveness of the strategy was significantly hampered by a **poor definition of youth homelessness** in the initial strategy and **inadequate information systems** for monitoring youth homelessness, a problem compounded by the inadequate definition. These have also hampered the planning and management of services.
- While there continues to be **widespread agreement with the content of the strategy**, stakeholders felt it suffered from having identified **too many actions**, none of which were prioritised.
- The ability to **access timely mental health and intellectual disability services** for children in crisis or out-of-home remains problematic in some areas.
- While there were some good examples of **interagency working**, this is an area where there is **potential for considerable improvement**.
- While there have been considerable **improvements in the range and quality of accommodation supports** for children, there remained **deficits in some places and a lack of flexibility** to meet different needs. Emergency residential hostels for children should be open throughout the day.
- There needs to be a greater understanding of the **needs of minority groups**, such as Travellers, ethnic groups and LGBT youth, **in relation to homelessness**.
- **Accessing services through Garda stations**, as the first port of call for first-time users of the service, is **inappropriate** and intimidating for many children, and a plan for stopping this practice wherever possible needs to be implemented.
- **Service responses for children aged 16-18 need renewed attention** since stakeholders felt they needed different responses to younger children and sometimes fell into the gap between services for younger children and adults.
- **Managing the transition between children and adult services across a range of agencies** needs to be improved and special attention needs to be given to young people aged between 18 and 25 years.
- Stakeholders felt there was the potential to improve support for children and young people in emergency accommodation to **remain and continue on in education.**

Recommendations for action

A number of recommendations emerged from the review. These relate to improving services for vulnerable children in relation to welfare, protection and risk of homelessness.

1. Governance and supporting effective multi-agency working

1.1 The Department of Children and Youth Affairs (DCYA) should be the lead Department in relation to the implementation of these recommendations as part of a planned engagement with the Departments of Health; Environment, Community, and Local Government; Education and Skills; Justice and Equality; and Social Protection; as well as the Health Service Executive (HSE), HSE Children and Family Services and the voluntary and community sector.

1.2 The DCYA should monitor the implementation of these recommendations.

1.3 Emerging Children's Services Committees should be tasked with supporting integrated and comprehensive service responses at a local level. Where there are existing effective local interagency groups addressing youth homelessness, they should integrate with working groups for children at risk under the Children's Services Committees.

1.4 HSE Children and Family Services should ensure that there is planned and proactive engagement and linkage with relevant services outside of its own remit so that children receive integrated service responses and therefore achieve the best possible outcomes.

2. Emergency and follow-on accommodation review

2.1 The use of Garda stations at night by children accessing emergency accommodation for the first time should be stopped. HSE Children and Family Services should be tasked with developing alternative responses wherever practical.

2.2 HSE Children and Family Services should ensure that emergency residential accommodation in Dublin remains open to children throughout the day.

3. Meeting the needs of older adolescents

3.1 HSE Children and Family Services should plan prevention and early intervention services where they are required to support at-risk children in the 16-18 age group.

3.2 HSE Children and Family Services should continue to monitor the use of Section 5 of the Child Care Act 1991 as a way of providing support to children who are 16 and 17 years of age.

3.3 The DCYA should engage with other Government departments to ensure integrated services across key agencies in terms of service plan development and operational policy.

4. Continued support

4.1 As set out in the current National Aftercare Policy, the assessment for aftercare services and provision of services should apply to children who have been supported by HSE Children and Family Services under Section 5 of the Child Care Act 1991.

4.2 All children (under 18 years of age) who are discharged from a detention school or prison should have an assessment of their aftercare needs undertaken and, where appropriate, an aftercare plan should be agreed with HSE Children and Family Services.

5. Education

5.1 Children who are out-of-home and at risk of dropping out of, or being suspended from, school should be flagged for particular attention by HSE Children and Family Services and Educational Welfare systems. Every effort should be made to ensure that those who are in temporary accommodation are assisted in attending school.

5.2 The DCYA should engage with the HSE and the Department of Education and Skills to address any unintended barriers to participation in third-level education by young adults who are homeless or at risk of homelessness, particularly those who are looking to re-enter education.

6. Transition to adult services

6.1 The DCYA should identify service implementation issues with HSE Children and Family Services and engage with other Government departments with responsibility for mental health services, education, disability, addictions and accommodation in relation to children who are in aftercare and with those who are in need of ongoing support as guided by the assessment of need by HSE Children and Family Services in transitioning to adult services.

6.2 The DCYA, in developing the new National Children and Young People's Policy Framework, should engage with other relevant Government departments to ensure that youth homelessness and the specific needs of 16-23 year-olds are addressed.

7. Information and evaluation

7.1 HSE Children and Family Services should provide clear information about services for vulnerable and at-risk children through its website and other available information outlets. This information should include responses for practitioners and the voluntary and community sector about children at risk of being out-of-home.

7.2 The DCYA should decide on revised definitions for 'youth homelessness' in consultation with relevant statutory and voluntary agencies.

7.3 The DCYA should continue to support building and expanding the evidence base on successful responses to taking action on or preventing youth homelessness within an overall context of achieving good outcomes for children.

CHAPTER 1:

BACKGROUND TO REPORT

1.1 Terms of Reference

In September 2011, the Centre for Effective Services (CES) was asked by the Department of Children and Youth Affairs (DCYA) to conduct a high-level review of the implementation of the Youth Homelessness Strategy, published by the Department of Health and Children in 2001.

Implementation has been described by Dr. Dean Fixsen and Dr. Karen Blase, Co-Directors of the National Implementation Research Network at the University of North Carolina, as 'the art and science of incorporating innovations into typical human service settings to benefit children, families, adults, and communities' (Fixsen and Blase, 2009).

Terms of Reference were agreed in November 2011 and work on the review began shortly before Christmas, with a meeting of a key stakeholder group on 16th December. The purpose of the review was:

- to establish the extent to which the strategy had been successful;
- to identify blockages and challenges to the implementation of the strategy;
- to make recommendations for a new implementation framework for the strategy.

In addition, it was agreed that the review would take an approach which addressed the following issues relating to scope and methodology:

- To utilise the 12 objectives of the strategy as headings under which judgements would be formed in relation to implementation of the strategy.
- To utilise the statistics in relation to youth homelessness in the context of a consideration of the definition of youth homelessness and the availability and suitability of information relating to youth homelessness.
- To consider what effect the strategy and any other factors have had on the numbers of youth homeless.
- To make use of the Health Service Executive's *Report of the National HSE Children and Family Services Working Group on Youth Homelessness* (HSE, 2008) and to consider to what extent this unpublished document can be used as a baseline, given the agreement among key organisations in relation to its findings.
- To inform the work of the review by referencing the 10 recommendations from the *Fourth Report of the Special Rapporteur on Child Protection* (Shannon, 2010).
- To consider the term 'youth homelessness' in terms of its usefulness within the context of policy and service delivery across a range of Government departments and organisations engaged with homelessness for children, families and adults.
- To engage with key stakeholders across a range of statutory and voluntary organisations.
- To give special consideration to the use of Section 5 of the Child Care Act 1991 as a means of providing accommodation to children who present as homeless, instead of using the provisions of the Act to receive the child into the care of the HSE.
- To ensure that while the focus of the strategy is on children under 18 years of age, that where relevant, issues in relation to young people over 18 years of age who have been in formal or informal care, and their subsequent aftercare should be referenced.

1.2 Methodology

In order to examine the implementation of the strategy, a number of sources were drawn upon. The review consisted of:

- a review of key documentation;
- a meeting with key stakeholders facilitated by the DCYA;
- semi-structured interviews with 23 key stakeholders, either individually or in groups (*see Appendix B for a list of participatory organisations*) and a meeting with the interagency Cork Youth Homelessness Forum;
- a web-based survey aimed primarily at front-line practitioners and service managers, for which 164 responses were received (*see Appendix B*);
- semi-structured interviews with service users;
- data from the HSE on the Crisis Intervention Service (Dublin) and Liberty House (Cork).

Interviews were recorded, transcribed and analysed by content analysis using NVivo software. Open-ended responses to the survey were similarly analysed and quantitative data were analysed using SPSS software. Key findings were synthesised and presented to stakeholders at a workshop in order to validate the analysis.

The review team received academic and quality assurance from Dr. Paula Mayock of the Children's Research Centre, Trinity College, Dublin, who has published extensively in this area.

1.3 Structure of report

Following this background to the report (including the Terms of Reference and methodology), the report is structured as follows:

- **Chapter 2** provides the context for the Youth Homelessness Strategy, published in October 2001. It also sets out the legal and services background to child welfare and children in care, and the current provision and demand for emergency services, including youth homelessness.
- **Chapter 3** presents the findings of the review, organised under the 12 objectives of the Youth Homelessness Strategy within the three strands of preventive measures (Section 3.2), responsive services (Section 3.3) and planning and administrative supports (Section 3.4). Under each strand, there is:
  - a review of key documentation;
  - an analysis of the facilitators of change identified by stakeholders or by the review team;
  - an analysis of the challenges to successful implementation in relation to that objective.
- **Chapter 4** presents the conclusions of the review.
- **Chapter 5** provides recommendations on the continuing implementation and monitoring of developments to support improved outcomes for children at risk of homelessness.

The report concludes with a list of **References** that informed the review and a number of **Appendices**, detailing various aspect of the study.

1.4 A note on terminology

In this report, the term 'children' is used to describe all children and young people aged 0-18 to reflect the statutory definition in current use. Although the strategy was called a *Youth* Homelessness Strategy, it related to those aged 0-18 only. Where the term 'young people' is used, it refers to those over 18 years.

CHAPTER 2:
INTRODUCTION AND CONTEXT

2.1 Children in need of care and accommodation

There are many reasons why children are unable to live with their parent(s) and family. They include neglect, domestic violence and abusive family situations, family conflict, family homelessness and parental difficulties in coping. Children who experience serious difficulties may develop problematic behaviour, such as school absence, aggression and substance misuse. Reasons for children being unable to live with their families and coming into State care, and the pathways by children into homelessness are broadly similar. Children have diverse profiles and family histories, and those who fall under the definition of 'homeless' may experience a range of conditions – from temporary or episodic leaving home to persistent homelessness.

Research has demonstrated that homelessness for children is not an isolated problem, but indicates a lack of safe adult care and a stable home base. Children who experience homelessness are more likely than their peers to have physical and mental health problems, and suffer from drug and alcohol misuse. Changing address and living in unstable accommodation makes accessing services more difficult and this can contribute to a downward spiral. Although the causes of becoming and remaining homeless are complex, poverty and social exclusion are factors common to the majority of children who experience homelessness. The need for prevention and early intervention – including family support and child welfare services, as in all child and family situations at risk – is widely acknowledged. In particular, a supported transition from child to adult services for children who are accommodated in emergency or short-term residential care/supported lodgings or in foster care is crucial to prevent young adults becoming homeless.

2.2 Service development for children

There have been significant improvements in the service response to youth homelessness in the last 10 years. Positive implications of the changed responses to youth homelessness can be deduced from the fact that it was a rare occurrence for children to be found during the 'rough sleeper counts' conducted by the Dublin Region Homeless Executive in Dublin county in 2010, 2011 and 2012.

The range and standard of services for children in need of care and support have improved over the past decade and this appears to have contributed to a decrease in the number of children accessing services through the homeless sector. The range and scope of family support services have also increased and where they are put in place, they are the first point of call for the majority of families under stress, with the aim of working with families before a crisis emerges. Children in need of emergency accommodation (including those who present as homeless) are assessed as children in need of welfare and protective services, and, depending on their age and location, are offered a foster care service, supported lodgings or residential unit.

For children in care, the percentage of placements in foster care has increased and now stands at 91%. Residential services are operating to improved standards, have better staff:child ratios and more specialised care planning and interventions. Specialist residential placements for children with challenging behaviour, including high risk-taking behaviour, have become increasingly available over the past decade in High Support Units, Special Care Units (the latter under the direction of the High Court) and individual placements. National standards for children's residential care (which includes emergency hostels) and foster services are in place for over a decade. HSE residential services and all foster care services are inspected by the Health Information and Quality Authority (HIQA) and these findings are published (*see SSI Inspection reports, available at:* www.hiqa.ie/social-care). The HSE inspects and registers residential services in the private and voluntary sectors.

Children aged 15-17 who come to the attention of emergency and youth homeless services as being vulnerable and at risk are typically more challenging to care for because they may be out of school; have experienced neglect and serious family discord; have mental health or learning difficulties; move amongst their peers' homes; and are less inclined to engage with social work services. Services need to provide early and flexible options to engage with these children and to support them beyond their 18th birthday.

On a broader basis, the ongoing 'change agenda' in HSE Children and Family Services will continue to impact on the structure and delivery of youth homelessness services in the future:

- The 'change agenda' aims to build a service model based on a cross-disciplinary and multi-agency approach to managing the child protection and welfare system, with clearer management and budgetary accountability, and better workforce planning, training and induction of new staff.
- The revised edition of *Children First: National Guidance for the Protection and Welfare of Children* (July 2011) provides greater clarity and guidance for individuals and organisations in identifying and responding appropriately to child abuse and neglect (DCYA, 2011).
- A single agency assuming statutory responsibility for services for children and families will be established in 2013, called the Child and Family Agency.
- A national review panel under independent chairmanship has been established to review serious incidents, including deaths of children in care and aftercare.
- The Health Information and Quality Authority (HIQA) has developed *National Standards for the Protection and Welfare of Children* (June 2012) and started inspecting HSE Child Welfare and Protection Services in November 2012 (HIQA, 2012).

Responses to children in need of care and protection, including homelessness

Under the Child Care Act 1991, the Health Service Executive (HSE) has a statutory duty to promote the welfare of children up to 18 years of age who are not receiving adequate care and protection. If a child is in need of care and protection and is unlikely to receive it at home, the HSE has a duty to ensure they receive appropriate care.

The first step, in most cases, following the identification of a child at risk is to, where appropriate, work with the parents and child to assist them by way of family support and therapy, parenting interventions, counselling, and mental health, addiction and other specialist services. Services for children that may be offered include family support, youth work, Garda Síochána diversionary services, school retention programmes and mental health services.

In cases where parents are unable to cope, due to illness or other serious problems, they may agree to their children being taken into the care of the HSE on a voluntary basis. In these cases, while the HSE has care of the children it must consider the parents' wishes as to how the care is provided. Over 60% of admissions to care in 2011 were on a voluntary basis. The HSE is obliged to provide care for these children for as long as their welfare requires it.

In cases where the HSE has serious concerns for the care and well-being of a child, and where it is not suitable or the parents are not agreeable to a voluntary care arrangement, the HSE may apply to the Courts for a Care Order.

Over 90% of children in care are placed in foster care on an emergency, short-term and long-term basis. In the first instance, the HSE seeks a suitable relative or person known to the child to provide relative care. Around one-third of children in foster care are with relatives. Children aged 12 and under are not placed in a residential setting unless for an agreed reason (e.g. to keep sibling groups together) and for the shortest time possible. Residential care is mainly provided in domestic houses, staffed by professionally qualified staff caring for, on average, 3-5 teenagers.

Section 5 of the Child Care Act 1991 provides that where it appears that a child is homeless and the HSE is satisfied that there is no accommodation available for the child within their extended family, and where the child is not being taken into care, the HSE shall make suitable accommodation available for him or her. The HSE's operational policy provides that Section 5 will only be used in exceptional circumstances where a child is aged 16 or 17. These children are accommodated either in a residential unit or supported lodgings, and are provided with a key worker and with general support.

It is contrary to HSE policy for children to be accommodated without a parent/guardian in a Bed and Breakfast (B&B).

Emergency services for children

Due to differing demand and historical organisational reasons, the emergency services have developed differently in the greater Dublin region, Cork City and the rest of the country.

The **Crisis Intervention Service** and the out-of-hours social work teams covering Dublin, Wicklow and Kildare provide initial assessment and accommodation services for children in emergencies and out of normal office hours. In the rest of the country, an **Emergency Place of Safety Service** is provided in response to children in similar situations, in partnership with An Garda Síochána. This applies to all emergencies, including a child saying they have nowhere to live. An emergency could occur for any of the following reasons: where a parent is rushed to hospital and a child has to be cared for; where a parent was found not to be in a fit state to care for a child; where a foster care or residential care placement breaks down in an unplanned way; where a teenager leaves home due to ongoing abuse or conflict; or where a separated child seeking asylum arrives at a national border outside of office hours.

There are currently two social work out-of-hours pilot sites in Cork and Donegal, with the plan to eventually develop a national out-of-hours service.

The emergency services are provided against a range of crisis situations, including homelessness. Unfortunately, the data published did not distinguish between the different reasons for referrals or the specific reason where a child is offered emergency accommodation. In addition, with the exception of one emergency residential hostel, in general the services that provide emergency accommodation also care for children for a range of reasons, for up to 6 months, and are operating to standards for a residential children's centre.

Improvements in emergency services have largely eradicated the need for children to be held in children's hospitals for social reasons. The services that have traditionally been called 'hostels' for youth homeless actually provide short-term/medium-term residential care to children and young people for a range of reasons.

Greater Dublin Region, Kildare and Wicklow

The **Crisis Intervention Service (CIS)** is run by the HSE Children and Family Services and provides an emergency out-of-hours service to children in the Dublin, Kildare and Wicklow areas. Its remit is to respond to crisis/emergency situations, whereby a child requires an immediate placement either due to child protection and welfare concerns, *or* due to placement breakdown because the home situation is unsafe or because they have been told not to return to their home. The CIS consists of a social work service accessible by emergency services, with accommodation consisting of emergency foster carers, supported lodgings and a dedicated residential hostel.

The CIS aims to prevent children from using emergency care unnecessarily. Where appropriate, CIS social workers place children with extended family members or friends, or mediate between children and parents where there has been a breakdown in relations. A child is placed in foster care, supported lodgings or an emergency residential unit only when other options with family and community have been exhausted. Children aged 12 years and younger are always placed with foster carers.

Referrals to the CIS are received by telephone from those emergency services that work at night and weekends, i.e. An Garda Síochána, hospitals, and ambulance services. Referrals that are accepted are where children are in need of care and accommodation, and include the immediate safety and welfare of children, children in crisis and children identified by the Garda National Immigration Bureau as separated children seeking asylum. Where a child is in residential or foster care and has an unplanned care placement breakdown, and a social worker cannot access a suitable alternative before close of working hours, a referral may be made by the social worker to the CIS to provide a placement.

Children who need emergency accommodation outside of office hours and who are known to the CIS may attend at a Reception Service in Lefroy House, a residential centre in Dublin, to meet with a social worker. Young people who are attending for the first time and are not known to services must go to a Garda station. From there, the out-of-hours social worker is contacted and travels to the Garda station to meet with the child and to assess their circumstances. The background to this practice is twofold: Garda stations are open 24 hours across a wide range of areas and the nature of the location provides personal security to the social worker while an initial assessment is undertaken, including whether it is safe for the social worker to drive the child during the night to emergency accommodation. Where possible, the social worker makes contact with the parents/guardians/family members to see if they can help with the situation and provide care for the child. In the event that emergency accommodation is considered the only immediate solution, parental permission is sought where possible. The social worker then brings the child to the emergency accommodation. All details of contacts with children during out-of-hours are passed to the local area social work team by the start of the following working day. The local social work team then takes responsibility for the case and will follow up on any further assessments or necessary interventions.

The CIS provides the following services for children out-of-home:

- An emergency social work service, available 7days a week between 6pm and 6am, and each Saturday, Sunday and public holiday from 9am to 5pm, all year round.
- A night reception centre to meet with the emergency social worker is located in Lefroy House in Dublin City Centre. It caters for children who need accommodation and who are known to the service. The reception centre is open from 5pm to 11pm.
- A panel of emergency foster carers who provide a place of safety for up to 3 nights for children.
- Emergency placement in supported lodgings for young people aged 16-17.
- 7 emergency beds at Lefroy House residential hostel on a night-by-night basis for boys and girls, aged 12-17, and one emergency placement available in Sherrard House girls' residential hostel.
- In 2011, the CIS had an additional 6 places in Grove Lodge in North Co. Dublin. This service closed down in mid-2012 and was replaced with a Fostering and Supported Lodgings Service. The maximum length of stay in these placements is 14 nights.

The CIS service has reported sufficient emergency places to meet demand in 2011 and 2012 to date.

The Lefroy House residential hostel has single rooms and children are provided with meals and a recreation space. It has a good level of staff support, with one-to-one immediate assessment of need, assistance with making and accompanying children to appointments, and contact with family and school, where appropriate. This residential hostel closes during the day and children may attend the Crisis Intervention Service Partnership (CISP). This is an outreach service delivered in partnership between CIS and Focus Ireland. The CISP team is available from 9am to 5pm, Monday to Friday, and offers the following services:

- Duty service: A duty worker follows up with the relevant social work department in relation to children who have been placed with the CISP.
- Intensive support for new clients: This involves meeting the child at the residential unit and either accompanying them to the relevant social work department or bringing them to the CISP for the day.
- Individual key working: Children are allocated a key worker.
- Supporting emergency foster/supported lodging placements during the day.

The CIS also has access to 18 medium-stay places in residential centres for children moving on from emergency accommodation. These centres historically catered for homeless children; however, this is not the case now since they are open to referrals from other services and provide the standard of care and welfare appropriate to residential centres. In addition, there are 7 aftercare support flats available to both young men and women, aged from 17½ years, for a period of 6 to 12 months.

Cork/Kerry Homeless Service for 15-17 year-olds

Liberty Street House in Cork is a dedicated service for children who are out-of-home or at risk of being so, and for older separated children seeking asylum. It is a social work-led service covering the areas of Cork and Kerry. The service is primarily aimed at adolescents, aged 15-18, who are out-of-home or at risk of being out-of-home. The focus of the service is on preventative and family support work so that children can be supported to remain in their homes. It provides social work and child care leader support to children who are out-of-home or in conflict situations in their family homes and at risk of leaving or being put out-of-home. The disciplines based at the service work together to ensure that the children benefit from a comprehensive range of services aimed at preventing family breakdown or re-integrating them with their families and community as quickly as possible. Staffing includes social workers and child care leaders, with access to a public health nurse working in the area of sexual health and pregnancy support. There is also a domestic violence social work service based in Liberty Street House in Cork, which works with female victims of domestic violence.

The Liberty Street service provides a transitional support service to young people over 18 years of age who continue to require accommodation, support and advice. A range of accommodation options are provided and managed by the service, including supported lodgings and semi-independent accommodation.

Referrals are received from the child protection teams, schools, a wide range of community-based services and also directly from children and families. All referrals are received by the duty social worker, who undertakes an immediate initial assessment. Following this assessment, if the referral is deemed appropriate for the service, the child is allocated a social worker or child care leader. The priority at all times is to return a child home. Where a child is unable to return home, there are a number of accommodation options available. Emergency accommodation is provided for boys in Pathways and girls in Riverview, both in Cork City. Children move on from the emergency accommodation to the other accommodation options managed by Liberty Street House. Accommodation providers have access to an on-call service at night provided by two local residential services. The service also provides a social work/child care leader on-call service at Bank Holiday weekends. Although the majority of the children attending Liberty Street House are not homeless, the service does not in general take children who are 16 and 17 years of age who are under formal care of the HSE, but accommodates them under Section 5 of the Child Care Act 1991; this approach has been found to facilitate enhanced working relationships with the families of the children. The service works closely with the local child protection teams where necessary.

Emergency accommodation for children across the country (excluding 16-17 year-olds in Cork and the Greater Dublin Area)

In 2009, HSE Children and Family Services established the **Emergency Place of Safety Service** (EPSS). They subcontracted its operation to Five Rivers Ireland, a private company providing foster and residential placements. Through the EPSS, Gardaí access an appropriate place of safety for children found to be at risk outside normal working hours. This is done under the provision of Section 12 of the Child Care Act 1991.

As with CIS (*see above*), the children who are the recipients of the service will include those who present as out-of-home and other emergency situations, including children whose parents are unable to care for them due to an accident, illness or incapacity, where a child has been abused and the situation cannot wait until office hours resume, or a separated child seeking asylum.

While the development of the EPSS increased the placement options available to An Gardaí Síochána, it did not address the need to provide an out-of-hours social work service. To deal with this problem, the HSE established out-of-hours pilot projects in Cork and Donegal in 2011, with a national Oversight Committee involving representation from HSE Children and Family Services at national level, the relevant service providers in the areas, An Gardaí Síochána and Five Rivers Ireland. The pilot projects aim to provide an on-call out-of-hours social work service for An Gardaí Síochána. Outcomes from the two projects are currently being reviewed and a plan to put an out-of-hours service on a national basis is being developed.

Aftercare service

All children with a care history with the HSE on reaching 18 years of age are entitled to an aftercare service based on their assessed needs. The HSE's *Leaving and Aftercare Services: National Policy and Procedure* was published in 2011 and an interagency Aftercare Implementation Group, led by the HSE, enacts the policy. Assessment for an aftercare service is undertaken before a young person reaches the age of 18 and services are provided from 18-21 years of age. The HSE policy allows for this to be extended up to 23 years of age to complete a course of education. For young people in aftercare undertaking education and training courses, there is ongoing HSE financial support available. Aftercare supports include the provision of advice, practical, social and emotional support, and accommodation. Young people who are unemployed are eligible for financial support from the Department of Social Protection. The HSE provides a 'once-off' financial support for young people leaving care and moving into private rental accommodation to allow them purchase necessary household items.

The HSE policy provides that a young person must have been in care for at least 12 months prior to their 18th birthday in order to be eligible for aftercare services, unless they are found to have had extensive experience of social work intervention throughout their childhood and teenage years.

Currently, children who have been accommodated under Section 5 of the Child Care Act 1991 are not entitled to access a statutory aftercare provision since they are not in the care of the State. The HSE provides an ongoing support plan for young people accommodated and supported under Section 5 on turning 18 years of age. The plan should be responsive and relevant to each young person's circumstances and should focus on supporting the young person's transition to independent living. The important requirements for young people on turning 18 are for secure, suitable accommodation, as well as further education, employment and/or training. These requirements should be prioritised in developing an ongoing support plan and should continue up to the age of 21, or where the young person is involved in a course of education until this course is completed.

2.3 Data on youth homeless

Examining the extent of youth homelessness is problematic because the data collated and published refer to all who are referred to and seek emergency accommodation, and do not distinguish between subgroups, including those who fall into the current definition of 'youth homelessness'. It is not possible to collect data accurately on those at risk of becoming homeless or to find common links to other jurisdictions.

Definition in Youth Homelessness Strategy

'Youth homelessness' is defined in the 2001 Youth Homelessness Strategy as:

> 'Those who are sleeping on the streets or in other places not intended for night-time accommodation or not providing safe protection from the elements or those whose usual night-time residence is a public or private shelter, emergency lodging, B&B or such, providing protection from the elements but lacking the other characteristics of a home and/or intended only for a short stay.'

Included within this meaning are 'young people who look for accommodation from the Eastern Health Board Out-of-Hours Service and those in insecure accommodation with relatives or friends regarded as inappropriate, that is to say where the young person is placed at risk or where he or she is not in a position to remain'.

This definition leads to data collection problems. For policy purposes, it is important to include children at risk of homelessness (e.g. having left home and staying temporarily with friends). However, their inclusion for data collection purposes poses challenges. In addition, since homeless services for children are a subset of emergency services, it is inaccurate to use data of demand or supply of emergency services as an indication of homelessness in children.

Over the course of the Youth Homelessness Strategy, the information available describing the numbers of referrals to emergency services has frequently been erroneously attributed to homelessness (without a parent or guardian) in children. The services described above (the Crisis Intervention Service and the Emergency Place of Safety Service) manage emergencies relating to children needing care and accommodation, including young homeless people, children where a residential or foster care placement breaks down as an emergency, and separated children seeking asylum.

What is clear is that the phenomenon of children sleeping rough has largely ceased. The demand for emergency residential hostel places for children due to homelessness has decreased in recent years, with hostel closures in Dublin, Limerick and Galway. Information produced in the earlier period of the strategy refers in the main to referrals for *all emergency services*, but this information was termed as 'homeless'. It indicated a static number of homeless presentations between 2001 and 2006, at around 450 per year. For the period between 2007 and 2010, the data were either incomplete or not published due to their poor quality. Data were collected locally to inform local service delivery.

Youth Homeless Contact Forms (YHCF) were introduced in 2004 to improve data collection. These were unsatisfactory due to unclear definition; confusion regarding reports of contact/referrals with services, rather than number of children; the complexity of the forms; and inconsistencies in completing them.

A new monitoring system for youth homelessness was implemented in 2011. It collected information on the number of children placed in emergency residential centres from the Emergency Place of Safety Service.

Statistics for children accommodated in a residential hostel, 2011

During 2011, a total of 245 children aged 12-17 were accommodated in emergency residential accommodation, primarily as a result of family relationship breakdown or a placement breakdown either from foster care or residential placement breakdowns (*see Table 1*).

A total of 131 children spent more than 4 consecutive nights in the accommodation. The remaining 48 children were placed for 3 nights or less.

The HSE region of Dublin North East was the location for the two residential hostels serving Dublin, Kildare and Wicklow – Grove Lodge (closed on 13 June 2012) and Lefroy House. HSE West closed its hostel in 2010 due to lack of demand. HSE South operates two residential centres that provide accommodation in Cork City for children out-of-home for a range of reasons.

Table 1: Number of children placed in emergency residential centres/units in 2011

2011	Number of children admitted
Dublin CIS residential services, Grove Lodge, Lefroy House and 1 place in Sherrard Street	179
Cork Liberty Street House residential services, Pathways and Riverview	66
Total	**245**

Source: Data provided by CIS and HSE.

Statistics published by the HSE (2011b) show that of the 179 referrals to CIS emergency accommodation, 14 were admitted as either seeking accommodation or being homeless, while 165 (92%) were referred as children being out-of-home due to family relationship breakdown or a placement breakdown either from foster care or residential placement breakdowns.

During the period January – September 2012, the HSE reported that only one child presented as homeless to the CIS, and in this case, the child's family was going through adult homeless services. In the same period, 124 children, aged 12-17, were placed across all types of CIS emergency accommodation. All but 36 children were placed under the Child Care Act 1991 and were therefore in the care of the HSE.

- 60 children were placed under Section 4 of the Child Care Act 1991 (where parents are unable to cope due to illness or other serious problems, they may agree to their children being taken into the care of the HSE on a voluntary basis).
- 22 children were placed under Section 12 of the Child Care Act (which provides for the Gardaí, in emergency situations, to remove a child to safety).
- 5 children were subject of a Full Care Order (Section 18 provides that in cases where the HSE has serious concerns for the care and well-being of a child, and where it is not suitable or the parent is not agreeable to a voluntary care arrangement, it may apply to the Courts for a Care Order).
- 1 child was subject to an Interim Care Order (the HSE may seek an Interim Care Order under Section 17 to allow for assessment or exploratory work to be completed).
- 36 children were accommodated under Section 5 of the Child Care Act (where it appears that a child is homeless, unless that child is received into the care of the HSE, the HSE shall take such steps as are reasonable to make available suitable accommodation for him).

It is interesting to note that while 14 children were returned as seeking accommodation or homeless, the CIS provided support and accommodation for 36 children under Section 5 of the Child Care Act 1991, which allows the HSE to provide accommodation where a child does not need to be in care. Under HSE operational policy, this applies to 16 and 17 year-olds as part of a flexible range of service options. Being supported under this Section of the Child Care Act does not necessarily mean that the youths under 18 years of age were homeless.

It is not unreasonable to assume that the increasing number of children in alternative care and/or accessing aftercare services includes children who would otherwise be homeless. The number of children in care has risen by 35% – from 4,424 in 2000 to 5,965 in 2010. The number of children accessing aftercare has risen by 34% – from 783 in 2005 to 1,046 in 2010. The increases in the number of children in care, and those accessing aftercare, is likely to be partly due to the increase in the child population over these years (the population of 0-17 year-olds increased by 13.4% between 2002[1] and 2011 (HSE, 2011b)). The percentage of children coming into care remains proportionate.

There are limitations to the data above since currently there are no nationally available figures on reasons for children accessing emergency services. The data also capture those children in receipt of a service, but do not reflect those children who could be at risk of homelessness and not known to services.

What is clear is that the Youth Homelessness Strategy was put in place at a time when there were insufficient places for children who presented as homeless and where children were sleeping rough. There has been a significant reduction in the demand for homeless services, which points to a significant downward trend in youth homelessness. The number of places for homeless children has been cut due to this reduction in demand. However, this does not lessen the vulnerability of the children presenting in an emergency or their immediate and long-term needs.

1 *See* http://census.cso.ie/Census/TableViewer/tableView.aspx?ReportId=1359

CHAPTER 3: FINDINGS

This chapter presents the synthesised findings of the review in relation to each of the 12 objectives of the Youth Homelessness Strategy. Section 3.1 examines the 5 objectives relating to preventive measures, Section 3.2 is concerned with the 3 objectives relating to responsive services and Section 3.3 examines the 4 objectives relating to planning and administrative supports. Under each objective, a review of documentation is summarised, followed by the facilitators and challenges to implementing the objective identified through consultation and research.

Throughout this chapter, quotations are given from various stakeholders involved in the consultation for this review of the strategy; these have been reproduced verbatim so as to retain the tone of the comments.

In the review of documentation for each objective, a number of key reports and reviews are regularly referred to and these, in summary, are (full details in 'References' at end of report):

- NCO (2003) *Youth Homelessness Strategy: Monitoring Report*
- Fitzpatrick Associates (2006) *Review of the Implementation of the Government's Integrated and Preventative Homeless Strategies* (sometimes referred to as the Smyth Report)
- HSE (2008) *Report of the National HSE Children and Family Services Working Group on Youth Homelessness*

3.1 Preventive measures

Objective 1: Family support and other preventive measures

Family support and other preventive services will be developed on a multi-agency basis for children and young people at risk of becoming homeless. In particular, this will incorporate a generic out-of-hours crisis intervention service and where necessary multi-disciplinary teams to target at-risk young people.

REVIEW OF DOCUMENTATION

Departmental documentation and monitoring reports in the first 5 years of the Youth Homelessness Strategy (up to 2005) indicate that, as well as a focus on youth homelessness, there was investment and activity in all the Health Board areas in relation to broad family support services that would contribute to preventing youth homelessness. The HSE (2008) *Report of the National HSE Children and Family Services Working Group on Youth Homelessness 2008*[2] suggests that there had been some impact on families with the most complex needs, some evidence of funding to the community and voluntary sector for 'difficult to engage' young people and an increased focus on young people at highest risk in the community (e.g. in care, leaving care, released from custody). Specialist adolescent teams were developed in Cork, but the 2008 Report of the Working Group is still calling

2 Referred to hereafter as the 2008 Report of the Working Group.

for multi-disciplinary teams to be set up to target children at risk, for example, addiction outreach. While it is clear that local arrangements for generic crisis intervention have been established across the country, the Ombudsman for Children (2012a and 2012b) and the Special Rapporteur on Child Protection (2010) continue to echo the concern of the 2008 Working Group – that a nationally integrated 'out-of-hours' social work service has not been established. While there has been progress against this objective in that there is emergency accommodation available nationally, it is difficult to see from the documentation if, at a policy and planning level, the necessary connections have been made between preventive services/measures and the other objectives within the Youth Homelessness Strategy.

CONSULTATION FINDINGS

Facilitators of improvement

- **Resources for preventive services:** Findings from the consultation for the present review of the Youth Homelessness Strategy indicate that a large amount of resources has been dedicated to family support interventions. Nearly half of survey respondents (44%) rated the adequacy of family services as 'adequate' or 'better'. Youth work services, such as youth cafés, crime diversion projects and early school-leaving projects, have also been heavily invested in. By positively engaging young people in youth activities, they are less likely to be at risk of homelessness. The strategy's emphasis on the critical role of these preventive measures was praised, but stakeholders considered that resources for preventive services need to be prioritised in the future.

  'There's so much work being done with families. I sit on a resource panel and ... you see the care plans and the list of interventions from the social work department and allied services. There's a huge amount of work done to try and keep kids out of homeless services.' [Service provider]

- **Early intervention:** Findings from the consultation indicate that there is a drive towards earlier intervention. In Galway, the homeless unit has closed down, which is believed to be due to increased family support and early intervention in the community. Staff may sometimes feel that early intervention work is not a priority, but it prevents situations in the home from escalating and becoming crises in the future.

- **Flexibility and ethos:** Stakeholders identified flexibility and ethos as elements that make preventive services more effective. The 'ability of the service to absorb and respond to need as presented' was deemed by a service manager to facilitate better outcomes. A child-centred ethos, consistency and a community-based approach were also highlighted as enabling positive outcomes.

- **Increase in social work services:** The increase in child protection social workers within communities was seen to have had a positive impact and has enabled social workers to be more responsive. Out-of-hours social work services were welcomed where they are in operation. There is one dedicated social work service to out-of-home youth operating in Cork City. Being a dedicated service seems to have enabled greater access to services and the labelling of the service as 'out-of-home' rather than 'homeless' has made it more identifiable for families and referring agencies, and less stigmatising for service users.

Challenges

- **Deficit in multi-disciplinary early intervention approaches:** Many stakeholders consulted felt that the majority of services are crisis-led or responding to crises, rather than adopting prevention and early intervention approaches. They felt there was a deficit in the availability of services to support families encountering difficulties with adolescents, respite services and support for family interventions. They also highlighted that it can be difficult to engage families in these services. Stakeholders noted that due to the large caseloads of social workers, it is difficult for them to allocate time to preventive work with families.

  'Multi-disciplinary work has been patchy. This has something to do with the fact that youth homelessness is not viewed in its proper context nor in the context of its causal factors, and thus the response to it continues to be responsive/crisis-led, rather than preventative.' [Service provider]

- **Lack of nationwide out-of-hours social work service:** Frustration with the lack of a nationwide out-of-hours social work service was highlighted by a significant number of stakeholders consulted. Nearly three-quarters of survey respondents (72%) – outside of areas where out-of-hours social work services are in operation and where the majority of cases requiring services occur (Dublin, Wicklow, Kildare, and Cork) – stated that they 'never' or 'rarely' had access to social work services out-of-hours.

  'It is my experience that if a situation arises where a young person finds themselves homeless and this happens after 4.30pm, there is NOBODY to help.' [Practitioner]

- **Deficit in support services for those at risk of homelessness:** Many of those consulted emphasized the need for more specialised support services for young people at risk of homelessness or to tackle the causes of youth homelessness. They stated that accessing services for young people with addiction problems and with psychological and behavioural problems can be very difficult. The profile of young people at risk of homelessness also changes over time and an awareness of changing profiles is needed in order to intervene in a preventative way. Those consulted pointed to other vulnerable groups whose risk of homelessness is poorly understood, such as Travellers, or Lesbian, Gay, Bisexual and Transgender (LGBT) youth. LGBT youth, who appear to be over-represented in the population of homeless young people in international studies, were not often identified as a group with particular needs by service providers consulted in this review, which may reflect a lack of understanding of the issues for this group.

Objective 2: Education

Schools will actively support children at risk of homelessness, e.g. truanting children and those who leave school early, using the structures proposed under the Education Welfare Act 2000.

REVIEW OF DOCUMENTATION

A key action within this objective was the establishment of a National Educational Welfare Board (NEWB), which was completed in 2002. The NEWB's proposed role included promoting school attendance, working with schools to address non-attendance and assisting students having problems in schools. With the exception of establishing the NEWB, Departmental documentation and monitoring/review reports consistently recognise this as one of the objectives where the least progress has been made. The 2008 Report of the Working Group concluded that:

- The main barriers to the full implementation of the education and training actions in the Youth Homelessness Strategy related to:
  - no shared approach to take advantage of the potential of education/training structures and initiatives;
  - inadequate local networking between providers across these sectors;
  - inconsistent approach to the inclusion of education/training inputs into care planning for children and young people out-of-home or at risk of becoming homeless.

Difficulties in effective interagency working between health and social care and education are not unique to Ireland, but remain an important element of any strategy aimed at tackling the risk of youth homelessness.

CONSULTATION FINDINGS

Facilitators of improvement

- **Establishment and work of the NEWB:** Some stakeholders highlighted the establishment of the National Educational Welfare Board (NEWB) and the introduction of educational welfare officers as a positive development. The newly established home–school liaison team in the NEWB was also welcomed. Some service providers coordinated well with the NEWB to identify education options for children and young people.

'NEWB are pretty good in terms of working with us and trying to identify other options for young people who are out-of-school.' [Service provider]

- **Alternatives to mainstream education:** Alternatives to mainstream education, such as Youthreach, were perceived to be supportive and accepting of young people with challenging needs.

Challenges

- **Remit of the NEWB:** Most stakeholders felt that the NEWB was substantially under-resourced and the caseload of the educational welfare officers was high; they, therefore, considered that the NEWB was not sufficiently resourced to identify children at risk. The NEWB also does not have a remit to work with children after they reach the age of 16 and therefore does not work with the majority of young people in education known to the youth homeless services.
- **Schools not referring children to the NEWB:** Some stakeholders noted that in their experience, some schools do not always refer children out-of-school to the NEWB. There can therefore be a lack of awareness and understanding of youth homelessness, or risk of same, in schools.
- **Difficulty accessing services for emotional and behavioural difficulties:** Emotional and behavioural difficulties are barriers to remaining in school. Many stakeholders emphasized that services for these difficulties can be hard to access. Waiting lists for Child and Adult Mental Health Services (CAMHS) and the National Educational Psychological Service (NEPS) can be very long. Another issue that arose from the consultation was that children with these problems can be prematurely suspended or expelled from school, without the provision of sufficient interventions; they can then feel rejected or become embittered towards the system.
- **Difficulty accessing education in transition to adulthood:** Both stakeholders and service users reported that once children out-of-home reach 18 years of age and they have not previously been taken into care, it can be extremely difficult for them to complete their second-level education or access third-level education. In order to access grants to remain in education, they need to be unemployed and access the job seekers' allowance. The application process for support was reported as complex and inconsistent, with variations in practice across the country.

  'As tough as it was for me to stay in education while going through all of this, somehow I done it, but it wasn't easy, and I can see how youths will drop out of education ... because all you're worried about is your next meal.' [Young person]

Objective 3: Supporting local communities

Local communities will be supported to assist children and young people at risk of becoming homeless and their families.

REVIEW OF DOCUMENTATION

This third objective of the strategy called for improved coordination of community development activities at a local level and their integration with youth homelessness strategies. From the available documentation and reports, it is clear that with the establishment of Youth Homelessness Fora in most areas, there was a degree of interaction with fora for adult homelessness and local authority structures. The 2008 Report of the Working Group (HSE, 2008) highlighted the need to clarify the relationship between Youth Homelessness Fora and Child Protection Committees, and the emerging Children's Services Committees. The 2005 *Report of the Strategy Group on Homelessness Policy to the Cabinet Committee on Social Inclusion* usefully links the Youth Homelessness Strategy with wider homelessness policy, but this is the only example of this type of reporting. This suggests that this type of focus was not sustained at the highest level and the available evidence suggests that this lack of consistent focus was mirrored at local level.

CONSULTATION FINDINGS

Facilitators of improvement

- **Local and community development:** Findings from the consultation indicate that local and community development agencies can contribute to reducing the risk of youth homelessness by empowering young people through the development of social skills, improving relationships with adults and connecting them with services.
- **Visibility of services:** It emerged from the consultation that where services for children and young people at risk of homeless are visible within the community, early identification of children and young people at risk and their referral to services from community members are facilitated. Service 'open days', to which key members of the community are invited and where other service providers can promote their services, were felt to be an effective way to improve visibility.

Challenges

- **More preventive services needed at community level:** According to the survey, there was a general consensus that there was a deficit in accessible family and community services in some rural areas. Services tend to be centralised in urban areas. The following quote is indicative of this sentiment:

  > 'The homeless services for young people [Liberty Street House] are excellent in Cork City. They are pro-active and respond quickly. However, I also work in Bantry and there are limited services available here.' [Practitioner]

- **More coordination with local and community development plans needed:** Stakeholders did not report a coordinated response to youth homelessness at a local level. Child, youth and family support services need to coordinate with local and community development services in order to provide a more integrated, holistic approach to meeting the needs of this specific group of at-risk adolescents.

Objective 4: Aftercare

Aftercare services for children and young people leaving foster care and residential care, and other services provided by a health board, such as supported lodgings and for those leaving centres for young offenders, will be strengthened so that children and young people are supported in making the transition to living independently or returning to their families.

REVIEW OF DOCUMENTATION

The documentation reflects the consensus that this is one of the objectives where there has been the greatest progress. Part of this has stemmed from recognition that many of the children captured in the statistics in the 2001 Youth Homelessness Strategy were not homeless, but either in need of being placed in care or had been put out of their current placement. The HSE 2008 Report of the Working Group agrees with the earlier 2006 report entitled *Review of Implementation of the Youth Homelessness Strategy by the Health Service Executive* (known as the Smyth Report; Fitzpatrick Associates, 2006), which pointed to the 'inequity in the provision of Leaving and Aftercare Services with widespread variation nationally', while recognising the 'considerable strides' made in a number of areas. The documentation makes particular reference to the Department of Health and Children's (2004) *Guidelines on the Development of an Aftercare Policy*, which were developed by the Youth Homelessness Strategy Monitoring Committee. In 2011, the HSE developed a *Leaving and Aftercare Services: National Policy and Procedure* and a HSE-led Implementation Group has been established, which is currently developing an implementation plan. It is also of note that children generally stay in their care placement until at least their 18th birthday, while in the past it was more common for adolescents to leave at 15, 16 and 17 years of age, particularly if they were in conflict with their carers.

A *National Policy and Procedure on the Use of Section 5 of the Child Care Act 1991* has also been developed (HSE, 2011c). This addresses the eligibility of children under Section 5[3] Orders to access aftercare and states that:

> 'An ongoing support plan should be delivered and implemented for every young person supported under Section 5 on turning 18 years of age. This plan should be responsive and relevant to each young person's circumstances and should be focused on supporting the young person to make the transition to independent living. This support should continue up to 21 years of age or where the young person is involved in a course of education until this course is completed. The ongoing supports and assistance to young people on turning 18 years of age should be available as appropriate to each young person's individual needs and circumstances.'

CONSULTATION FINDINGS

Facilitators of improvement

- **Improvement in aftercare provision:** There have been great strides made in the improvement of aftercare provision over the last few years and many stakeholders acknowledged 'significant improvements since 2001'. The publication of the *Report of the Commission to Inquire into Child Abuse* in 2009 (known as the Ryan Report) also gave impetus to the improvements. Stakeholders considered that the actions in the Youth Homelessness Strategy in relation to aftercare were comprehensive and progressive for the time. A financial investment has been made in aftercare services. There are now 42 full-time aftercare posts, in addition to aftercare workers in voluntary agencies. There is a growing recognition that aftercare is a key component of the care system and it has been accepted as best practice. The vast majority of children in aftercare services remain in their foster placements, supported financially by the HSE. Those in residential care in the main either move to supported accommodation or to private rental premises.
- **Aftercare Implementation Group for national policy on aftercare:** The national policy on aftercare developed by the HSE Children and Family Services (2011) was seen as a very 'positive development'. A multi-disciplinary coordinated approach is being adopted and strong links between housing authorities, mental health services, disability services and primary care are being fostered.

Challenges

> 'A lot of work is being done for these kids; I still think there's a massive amount more that could be done.' [Service provider]

- **Inconsistency in aftercare provision:** While much progress has been made in relation to aftercare, it was felt by many stakeholders that there had been, or still was, inconsistency in provision across the country, with inadequate resources to achieve consistent provision. A lack of a specific budget for aftercare was highlighted and some service providers had experience of children in the past without aftercare support plans. There was also a degree of lack of awareness about the proposed changes to aftercare policy currently being developed by the HSE. Tighter budgets in recent times have meant that little semi-independent accommodation is being developed. Many children have little option beyond private rented accommodation and accessing rent allowance, thereby increasing their vulnerability. There are also structural barriers to accessing aftercare support when children move to other parts of the country.

  > 'It's not being resourced, and without that I don't know how well it will be implemented. It's very ad-hoc, it's inconsistent, it depends where you live, it depends if you have a social worker, if you have an aftercare plan.' [Service provider]

---

3 Section 5 states: 'Where it appears that a child in its area is homeless, the health board shall enquire into the child's circumstances, and if the board is satisfied that there is no accommodation available to him which he can reasonably occupy, then, unless the child is received into the care of the board under the provision of this Act, the board shall take such steps as are reasonable to make available suitable accommodation for him.'

- **Eligibility for aftercare provision:** Many stakeholders highlighted the need for statutory aftercare provision to be widened to include children not in care but accommodated under Section 5 of the Child Care Act 1991 (*see above*). These ineligible children can have significant difficulty accessing welfare and educational supports, which increases their vulnerability to homelessness.

  > 'I've just struggled because I didn't fit into any of the boxes and it's been my biggest struggle up until this day ... my brothers and myself just totally avoided care because when you're younger, you're just told bad stories about care ... I always say to myself to this day when I'm filling out forms, why did I not go into care because it would have been almost easier for me.' [Young person]

  Although the National Aftercare Policy (HSE, 2011a) and the National Policy and Procedure on the Use of Section 5 (HSE, 2011c) include these children within eligibility criteria for aftercare supports, there was concern among stakeholders that this would not be implemented in practice due to insufficient resources. There was some difference in views expressed among stakeholders about the issue of eligibility for aftercare provision for children arriving in Ireland separated from their parents, on reaching 18 years of age, when they are provided with Direct Provision Services by the Department of Justice and Equality while their application to remain in the State is processed. Stakeholders also raised the issue of children in the care system for frequent but short-term stays.

  The HSE stated that it would be inaccurate to say that children seeking asylum do not get aftercare. They are provided with accommodation by another arm of the State, i.e. the Department of Justice and Equality. Aftercare workers are allocated to those who are assessed as needing aftercare, to provide emotional support. It is Government policy that those seeking asylum can access support from the State through the Direct Provision system only, but it is not mandatory.

  Aftercare is provided to children who have experienced a substantial period of time in care. The National Aftercare Policy (2011) also states: 'It is accepted that there may be circumstances in which services are provided where a young person has been in care for less than a minimum period of 12 consecutive months prior to their 18th birthday, but have had extensive experience of care and ongoing intensive social work intervention throughout their childhood and teenage years.'

- **Need for flexibility in access to aftercare provision:** Children can find the transition from intensive support and 24-hour care to independent life very difficult. Those with learning disabilities and mental health difficulties are particularly vulnerable. Leaving care can also trigger depression and non-adaptive coping behaviours can develop. Stakeholders considered that young people needed to be able to dip in and out of aftercare support in their early 20s. Some young people may not engage with their aftercare plan and if they encounter difficulties a few months down the line, it is difficult for them to re-engage with aftercare services. The National Aftercare Policy states that young people who disengage will be monitored through telephone calls and letters for up to one year; however, they can re-engage at any time up to 21 years of age. Some stakeholders felt this age limit needed to be extended.

- **Inadequate provision for young people leaving criminal detention:** In addition to children and young people in care, the strategy also identified children and young people leaving centres for young offenders as being vulnerable to youth homelessness. Over three-fifths of survey respondents (62%) felt that the needs of children and young people being discharged from criminal detention were being poorly met or not at all. Where step-down facilities for young offenders were established and resourced, they are now no longer in operation and there is a 'gap' in terms of meeting the needs of this group. Many stakeholders felt that higher levels of structure and support are needed for this group at risk of homelessness.

The Irish Youth Justice Service (IYJS) stated that the current emphasis is on re-integration and the provision of support services within their community. The new Assessment Consultation and Therapy Service (ACTS) team being put in place will provide a mediation role in the transition from the child detention school to the home. The IYJS also felt that the recently agreed protocol for working with social work should mean that there is better support for children in care and with allocated social workers while they are in detention and afterwards.

It seemed that some stakeholders were not aware of planned changes or developments in relation to this group of children and young people, and that improved communication about these changes would be helpful.

3.2 Responsive services

Objective 5: Emergency responses

Emergency responses will be provided promptly to children and young people who become homeless; these services will be accessible and acceptable to this client group. Specialised 24-hour Reception Services will be provided in cities where appropriate.

REVIEW OF DOCUMENTATION

Monitoring and review of the Youth Homelessness Strategy up to 2005 show that all Health Board areas were addressing the matter of emergency responses, with the greatest progress being made in urban areas (Dublin and Cork) where there was the greatest need. With lower numbers and larger geographic areas, Health Boards in largely rural areas developed more flexible responses based on existing social work and care services. The 2008 Report of the Working Group suggests that disparities in funding and managerial capacity between Health Board areas negated 'a truly national approach'. It cites a study by Mayock and Carr (2007), who reported that 'the study's newly or recently homeless reported fewer living situations since the time they left home and most had little or no contact with a network of street-based homeless youth'. This indicates an improved response in more recent years. Further progress is identified, with children accessing emergency and homeless out-of-hours services reporting prompt access to services and an extensive range of supports, once again supported by findings from Mayock and Carr's study (*ibid*).

Drawing on *Planning for Children – Improving access to services for children in private emergency accommodation in Dublin* (O'Flynn and Chaloner, 2006), the 2008 Report of the Working Group notes the need for a more coordinated and holistic approach to the emergency accommodation needs of homeless families, particularly 'greater communication, cooperation and integration … amongst all the agencies and personnel working with homeless families'.

CONSULTATION FINDINGS

Facilitators of improvement

- **Improved access to emergency accommodation:** Many stakeholders agreed that access to emergency accommodation has improved. Half (51%) of direct service providers to under-18s felt the supply was adequate or good. The competition (or 'lotto' as some described it) for emergency beds, which was commonplace a decade ago, no longer exists. The emergency response to children under 12 was seen to be particularly good and these children generally stay a maximum of 3 nights with emergency foster carers. Survey respondents who were practitioners working directly with children and young people were more likely to perceive that emergency services had improved, compared to those who were not working directly with young people.

> 'I think what works well is that there is an immediate response and there is availability of beds ... and it's not the way it used to be where you're more street smart so you stay out tonight and a more vulnerable kid gets a bed. Everyone has a bed.' [Service provider]

- **Decentralisation in Dublin:** The decentralisation and combining of two emergency accommodation hostels from Dublin City Centre to Grove Lodge in Portrane was felt by some stakeholders to have had a positive impact. They felt that being outside of the city centre meant that there were not as many opportunities to engage with peers in anti-social behaviour. The large input from social work services and the prompt development of care plans were also viewed positively. However, this view was not shared by all (*see 'Challenges' below*). Grove Lodge closed in the summer of 2012 due to the nature of the building and lack of emergency demand.
- **Immediate response:** An immediate response and a focus on enabling the child to go back home or stay with other members of their family before considering accessing emergency accommodation options were seen to be the most effective responses. As one service provider commented, 'It is critical that beds are turned over and there's huge momentum on keeping beds moving to be able to meet demand'.

Challenges

- **Appropriateness of emergency accommodation questionable:** The appropriateness of one of the emergency accommodations was questioned, particularly in Dublin City Centre. The lack of 24-hour provision of residential care was seen to be inappropriate. Service providers reported that previous service users can hang around these accommodations and prey on the vulnerability of younger children. Foster care and supported lodgings were viewed as being more suitable. However, the challenge of appropriately placing children and young people who are under the influence of drugs and/or alcohol and who may be exhibiting challenging behaviour was highlighted.
- **Emergency accommodation not provided locally:** Many responses during the consultation indicated a lack of appropriate emergency placements within children's local areas for older at-risk teenagers or those not suitable for foster care. This probably reflects a wider ongoing debate about if and how specialist services, such as mental health and addiction services, can best be made available in each local area. There was variation in the adequacy of supply across the country and over three-quarters (76%) of respondents outside of Dublin and Cork rated the supply as 'poor' or 'none'. As discussed above, the decentralisation of emergency accommodation in Dublin was viewed very positively by some, but others felt it had unintended, negative consequences. Having a service too far from children's communities was considered to act as a barrier to accessing it: 'They don't want to be stuck out in the sticks', as one practitioner put it. Although emergency placements should be short-term, difficulties in accessing move-on accommodation options (*see 'Challenges' under Objective 7)* means that children can be away from their communities for weeks.
- **Accessing emergency services through Garda stations is inappropriate:** Garda stations are currently the designated access route to emergency accommodation services out-of-hours (although children are often in contact with services already and may present directly to them). This was considered to be inappropriate and intimidating for children, particularly for younger children and those with a history of criminal behaviour. Most stakeholders agreed that a better alternative was needed. However, the use of Garda stations as an access route was viewed more positively outside of Dublin.

Objective 6: Comprehensive needs assessment

A comprehensive assessment of children and young people who become homeless will be carried out as the basis for individual action/care plans for case management/ key working with the young person where necessary.

REVIEW OF DOCUMENTATION

Both the 1999 and 2011 editions of *Children First: National Guidance for the Protection and Welfare of Children* provide guidance in relation to assessing the needs of children who may be homeless. In 2002 and 2003, the National Children's Office (NCO) and the Youth Homelessness Strategy Monitoring Committee (YHSMC) attempted to collate in detail the actions of each Health Board in relation to all the actions contained in each objective of the Youth Homelessness Strategy. This is the only record of such an exercise being attempted and there no evidence to suggest it was repeated.

For this objective, in common with all the others, there is patchy reporting from the Health Boards. There is evidence of some progress, but in many cases there is no evidence one way or the other. The difference for this objective is that it is not picked up in detail in subsequent reports or reviews. From the Department of Health and Children documentation, it is not possible to say how well this objective has been met, although like preventative services (*see Section 3.1 above*), it is likely that improvements have been driven by generic improvements to the wider assessment of children's needs. The 2008 Report of the Working Group noted that newly or recently homeless youth reported 'fewer living situations since the time they left home', which could be an outcome of improvements to assessment. The Working Group also recommended that there was a need to develop a national common assessment model for the assessment of need.

CONSULTATION FINDINGS

Facilitators of improvement

- **Consistent assessment of needs in some services:** Findings from the consultation indicate that across service providers, there is variation in the assessment and management of children and young people's needs. A comprehensive assessment of children and young people's needs 'happens in some particular services', according to one service provider. Where it occurs, care plans are developed on the basis of these assessments and are regularly reviewed.
- **Staff skilled at identifying needs:** Those consulted indicated that many staff working in homeless services are considered to be highly experienced and capable of completing an appropriate needs assessment fairly quickly. The difficulty appears to be with accessing the specialist services required (*see 'Challenges' below*). It is easier to access support services when children are previously known and linked in to support services.

Challenges

- **Lack of standardised comprehensive assessments:** Stakeholders reported that adequate assessments and follow-on care plans are not always provided, leading to inequity in provision. In the survey, when service providers to homeless children were asked to rate the frequency at which comprehensive multi-disciplinary assessments involving specialist services were conducted, only 10% claimed they 'always' occurred. Although almost one-third (30%) claimed they 'usually' were conducted, about the same proportion (35%) claimed they were 'only sometimes' conducted and the remaining 25% said they were 'rarely' or 'never' carried out.
- **Lack of a holistic approach to needs assessment:** Findings from the consultation indicate that needs assessments tend to be focused on basic and accommodation needs, rather than on a more holistic approach and addressing the reasons for the child being out-of-home. Assessments also tend to be deficit-based, rather than focusing on children's strengths. Many stakeholders indicated that while the accommodation need is the most immediate need and is hugely important, it is only 'the first step'.

- **Lack of detection of mental health difficulties and intellectual disabilities:** The lack of detection and provision of support for mental health difficulties and intellectual disabilities, particularly mild learning disabilities, was emphasized in the consultation. This can contribute to challenging behaviour, which may not be recognised or understood. Three-quarters of survey respondents (75%) felt that the needs of children with mental health difficulties were being poorly met or not met at all. Service providers reported that children with intellectual disabilities can be bullied and taken advantage of by their peers in group residential settings, and are not sufficiently supported in developing the skills necessary for independent living. Nearly one-half of survey respondents (49%) felt that the needs of children with an intellectual disability were being poorly met, while 11% felt they were not being met at all.

Objective 7: Accommodation options

A range of accommodation arrangements will be provided for children and young people who are unable to return home as part of an integrated response to the child's needs.

REVIEW OF DOCUMENTATION

Reports and reviews to 2005 show a number of initiatives across the Health Boards, but reporting is patchy and given different reporting frameworks across the Boards, it is difficult to judge the extent of progress in this initial period of the strategy. By 2008, the HSE Report of the Working Group is still noting the need to ensure the separation of young adult care-leavers from other children and there is a greater focus on the different needs of men and boys. Reporting reflects the differences between urban areas, where specific services are developed, and the loss of focus on these issues in rural areas, where numbers of homeless children are low. The Review Team understands that national policies on supported lodgings were developed in 2012 and are being implemented by the HSE Children and Family Services.

CONSULTATION FINDINGS

Facilitators of improvement

- **Improvement in accessing accommodation options:** Consultation findings indicate that there has been an improvement in access to accommodation and also a greater range of options, particularly in urban centres. The improvement was attributed to a number of positive developments, including an increase in social workers, more supported accommodation, a greater range of types of residential placement and an increased supply of private residential services. The implementation of immediate responses was viewed by those consulted as being 'most successful'.

  Where resource panels and integrated structures for discussing accommodation needs exist, as in Cork City, access appears to be speedier, particularly when meetings are held at a frequency of at least every 2 weeks and when senior management from all accommodation options are represented.

- **Supported accommodation for older adolescents:** Stakeholders stated that a number of accommodation services were deemed to be 'excellent', particularly supported accommodation options. Supported accommodation was viewed by Cork stakeholders as the preferred option for the 16-18 age group who did not require more intensive placements with therapeutic inputs, since they may not need a full care setting but do need some support that is vetted. However, stakeholders also felt that it remains the case that for some 16-18 year-olds, being taken into care is in their best interests and it is vital that comprehensive and integrated services exist to support that.
- **Continuum of support in transition to adult services:** Providing a continuum of support, particularly in the transition from child to adult services, was emphasized in the consultation as being very important for the outcomes of children. Access to good-quality supported accommodation, private rented accommodation and tenancy

sustainment were viewed as being necessary to prevent adult homelessness. In some areas, the development of links between child and adult services has enabled the appropriate transfer of children where necessary. Having an interagency group dedicated to providing for the needs of 18-25 year-olds (such as the one coordinated by Cork City Council) was considered 'a great success in respect of sharing resources' and in accommodating young adults appropriately. This interagency group potentially provides a model for further interagency working, particularly in relation to managing the transition from youth to adult services.

> 'It's about putting our heads all together and coming up with something for that person.' [Service manager]

Challenges

- **Delay in accessing move-on accommodation options:** For a small number of young homeless people placed in emergency accommodation, findings from the consultation indicate that there can be a great delay in accessing move-on accommodation options. While just over one-third of survey respondents (34%) felt that speed of access was 'adequate' or 'good', the majority (66%) felt it was 'poor' or 'very poor'. The 'system is really slow sometimes' and children can become 'stuck' in it, as one practitioner commented. Placements are not always readily available and when they are available, the admission process can take weeks.

- **Limited range of appropriate accommodation options:** While the consultation indicates improved access to accommodation, most responses indicate a limited range of accommodation options for children with the appropriate levels of support needed. While the range of accommodation options is better in urban areas, stakeholders reported that the supply of foster care can be poorer, particularly for older adolescents with challenging behaviour. In Dublin and Cork, only one-quarter of survey respondents rated the supply of foster care as 'adequate' or 'better', compared to one-half of respondents in the rest of the country. Some stakeholders felt that more foster care could be provided if families were offered enhanced support. In addition, it was felt that placements with relatives were underutilised, although Ireland has, by international standards, comparatively high use of this option for children.

  > 'What a lot of them need isn't a residential bed, it's a supported lodging or a foster placement, and a foster placement who is able to cope with, not a little blond 3-year-old but a knarky 15-year-old stroppy girl - drunk - who's coming in late and has an older boyfriend, but yet is crying out for a family setting to help her put the structure on her life ... Residential is not normal, it's not a normal way to rear children. I think the exposure the children are having now to terrible behaviour in residential care would really alarm any of us.' [Practitioner]

- **Challenges in providing locally based accommodation:** Placement options can be located outside the areas of children's homes, thereby making it difficult to maintain links with their community and remain in school. When survey respondents were asked to rate the frequency at which they considered children were placed within their local communities, only 10% claimed they were 'usually' placed within their local communities; just over one-half (52%) stated they were 'sometimes' placed locally and the remaining 38% claimed they were 'rarely' or 'never' placed locally.

- **Difficulty transitioning to adult services:** The consultation responses emphasized that there are limited options available for 15-18 year-olds, particularly foster placements, and that children approaching their 18th birthday are not prioritised. Some young people may not be ready to leave the service once they reach the age of 18 and are in need of support up to the age of 25. Developments in aftercare provision were seen as very positive for those in receipt of formal care, but there were concerns for those who were not. While coordination with local authorities was reported to be occurring in some areas of Ireland, it was generally considered to be very difficult for single young adults to access local authority accommodation. Some may choose private rented accommodation, but may not be adequately prepared for independent life. There is evidence in the

Irish context that many who first experience homelessness as teenagers subsequently access adult homeless services. Recent changes in social welfare supports for the 18-24 age group were viewed as impacting very negatively on young people who experience housing instability and as acting as a barrier to young people exiting homelessness.

In the 2010 Budget, the Job Seekers Allowance was cut from €188.00 to €100.00 for young people who are 18-21 years of age. Young people aged 22-24 receive a payment of €144.00. If a young person has a history of State care, they are exempt from these cuts and receive a full payment. However, many young people in the 18-24 age range who experience homelessness do not have a history of State care. The rate at which a single person can claim Rent Allowance has also been reduced over the course of 2010-11 and a single person can currently claim a maximum of €475.00 per month.

> 'That 18 age is such an arbitrary figure. Looking at how society has changed significantly, nobody leaves home at 18 now. Young people are sitting their Leaving Certificate at 19. Risk factors for young people don't change because of a magic birthday.' [Service provider]

Objective 8: Meeting the needs of young people

A range of supports will be provided to meet children's health, educational and recreational needs based on each child's action/care plan and aimed at reintegrating the child into his/her community as quickly as possible.

REVIEW OF DOCUMENTATION

Reviews and reports on the implementation of the Youth Homelessness Strategy provide little detail on developments in this area. In one case, the Health Board connects initiatives under this objective with its interventions under Objective 1 (family support and other preventive services). Effective and targeted provision in this area would depend on the type of comprehensive needs assessment envisioned in Objective 6. Given the lack of information on assessment aimed specifically at young homeless people, it is not surprising perhaps that there is a lack of clarity in relation to provision under this objective. In addition, successful implementation of this objective would be closely related to education and training actions under Objective 2 and it is clear from the reports and reviews, including the 2008 Report of the Working Group, that education and training is an area that still requires considerable attention. Access to advocacy was an action under this objective, but by 2008 there was still a lack of clarity among service providers in relation to what 'advocacy' meant in this context.

CONSULTATION FINDINGS

Facilitators of improvement

- **Shared responsibility:** Findings from the consultation indicate that the needs of children out-of-home, like all children at risk and in care, are best met when there is shared responsibility for their needs. This appears to be facilitated by good coordination between practitioners, joint needs assessments, integrated service planning arrangements and interagency fora.
- **Holistic, strengths-based approaches:** Holistic approaches that are focused on building strengths and resiliency were highlighted in the consultation as being effective. Building children's confidence and life skills was reported to help prevent future episodes of homelessness.
- **Family-focused services:** Services that work preventively and with the family were perceived to be beneficial. Staff being respectful of the family's culture was also considered to be important, for example, when working with the Traveller community.
- **Flexibility:** Flexible and responsive services to individual needs were reported to be most effective. For example, the divide between child and adult services is removed in the case of women's domestic violence shelters so that children can access the most

appropriate services for their needs. These shelters accommodate mothers with children and young women experiencing domestic violence, and provide the most appropriate support for children in this situation.

- **Access to recreational facilities:** Service providers and service users alike greatly valued children having access to recreational facilities, such as gym memberships. However, nearly one-half of survey respondents (48%) felt that the recreational needs of young homeless people or those at risk of homelessness were being poorly met or not met at all. Resourcing recreational activities was not perceived to be expensive and increased resourcing would be very beneficial.

Challenges

- **Well-trained staff:** Well-trained staff were considered key to providing for the needs of children. Thousands of employed staff and volunteers have been trained in the use of *Children First* (DCYA, 2011), which national guidance is concerned with the recognition, reporting and management of child protection and welfare concerns. Training for staff regarding intellectual disability, mental health difficulties and sensitive issues such as sexual orientation and exploitation was reported to be very valuable.
- **Lack of integrated services:** Findings from the consultation indicate that youth homeless services are not integrated well with other services and, as a consequence, children's health, educational and recreational needs are not being met sufficiently. Some remarked that certain services were 'passing the buck' in relation to their responsibility for service provision. In particular, services for addiction, intellectual disabilities and mental health difficulties were highlighted as being very difficult to access, potentially leading to negative outcomes. Service providers reported being commonly told by mental health services that they could not work with children until they are in a secure environment, but this is not possible without a proper assessment and diagnosis. Difficulties accessing mental health services were emphasized for 16-18 year-olds, who appear to 'fall in the gap' between child and adult services. Situations were reported to have reached crisis point before interventions are provided and earlier intervention is necessary.

  '... they're lost, sometimes they're misdiagnosed. It's only when they do something really bad to somebody else or to themselves that eventually everything is thrown at them and it's not preventative, it's response-led.' [Practitioner]

- **Managing challenging behaviour:** The needs of children out-of-home are complex and some present with challenging behaviour. If a child in residential care is very aggressive, they may be placed in the emergency services while the situation is reviewed or an alternative placement is sought. Although it is against policy, children were reported to remain in emergency accommodation for 'months and months on end' because no suitable placements were found. Stakeholders perceived that boys tend to be barred from services more quickly than girls due to their overt aggressive behaviour, while girls are more likely to engage in more covert self-harming behaviour. It was also reported that children can be quickly labelled, with appropriate assessment, as exhibiting 'inappropriate behaviour', thereby making it very difficult to access services. Some service providers felt that residential care staff need to be better supported in understanding and managing challenging behaviour and that intervention models that have been demonstrated to be effective should be adopted. Broadening the recruitment of staff to include candidates from local communities with whom the children can relate was also recommended.

  'It's about maybe demanding high level of skills from our staff and giving them the skills to do it ... it's easy to shy away from these kids ... but they can be worked with.' [Service provider]

- **Unsafe or inappropriate environments:** Those consulted indicated that exposure to other service users, including those with challenging behaviour, drug use and the experience of peer pressure, can be detrimental to children using the services. In one emergency residential hostel, children have to leave in the morning because the unit does not provide a 24-hour service and children who are unwell are unable to remain in bed. Some accommodation options are not conducive to individual client work and it can be difficult to balance the specialised needs of individuals with the needs of others accessing that service. Three-quarters of survey respondents (76%) felt that the range of accommodation options available to meet the individual needs of children was 'poor' or 'very poor'. Stakeholders considered first-time placements should not be in group residential settings, but in alternative accommodation, such as foster care or supported lodgings. It was also felt that more support was needed to ensure first-time placements are successful, to prevent placement breakdowns and cycles of homelessness. In the period since the consultation took place, a greater range of services has been made available, including supported accommodation and foster care services.

- **Needs of minority groups need to be improved:** Minority groups, including children and young people from the Traveller community, ethnic minorities and young LGBT people, have particular needs, but stakeholders identified that these needs are not well understood by staff and little evaluation or monitoring has been conducted to examine their needs. Approximately one-third of survey respondents claimed they did not know how well the needs of these minority groups were being met.

3.3 Planning and administrative supports

Objective 9: Interagency coordination

Health boards are responsible and will take the lead role in implementing the Youth Homelessness Strategy in their area; effective arrangements for coordination with both statutory and voluntary service providers will be put in place.

REVIEW OF DOCUMENTATION

The key action under this objective was the establishment of Youth Homelessness Services fora. By 2004, fora had been established in 7 out of the 8 Health Board areas, with only the Western Health Board (WHB) not establishing a forum. The Southern Health Board (SHB) only established its forum in 2004 and by this time, the forum in the South Eastern Health Board (SEHB) had been disbanded and there was uncertainty about the future of the North Eastern Health Board (NEHB) fora. By 2012, only one forum was still functioning – in Cork and Kerry (i.e. in the former SHB area). The review by Smyth (2006) notes that:

> 'The efficacy of fora and their governance arrangements is variable reflecting and influenced by a plethora of issues encompassing resources including historical inequities in the system, significant variations in homelessness between urban and rural divides, managerial capacity and reconfiguration, with concomitant upheaval of community care based on family support services in a number of Boards. This process has been further compounded by health service reform.'

Different funding priorities, the variations in level of need between urban and rural areas, and competing demands on members' time, particularly a 'proliferation of committees within child care and protection services', also contributed to the reasons why this objective was not delivered. Without effective fora in place at Health Board level, it was extremely difficult to develop a truly national approach to the issue of youth homelessness. In 2006, Smyth echoes the National Children's Office's Monitoring Report from 2003, which said that 'it must be acknowledged that the plans were written in a more positive economic climate'. This and the other observations by Smyth were endorsed in the 2008 Report of the Working Group (HSE, 2008).

The Youth Homelessness Strategy suggested that a possible action under this objective would be to establish the fora as part of arrangements for the Child Protection Committees, although there is no evidence to indicate whether any Health Board area ever took this approach. By 2008, the Working Group was concerned about duplication between Child Protection Committees and the emerging Children's Services Committees, suggesting that the Youth Homelessness Fora might find their natural home within the latter. Both the 2008 Working Group and the 2010 Special Rapporteur on Child Protection suggested that there was still a need to strengthen links with adult homelessness policy, service provision and fora.

CONSULTATION FINDINGS

Facilitators of improvement

Stakeholders acknowledged the considerable progress made to date, while continuing to identify deficits and push for improvements in interagency coordination.

- **Structures to facilitate interagency working:** A number of current structures were reported to be facilitating interagency working, including resource panels, Children's Services Committees and a Youth Homelessness Forum operating in Cork and Kerry. Over one-third of survey respondents rated the coordination of agencies as 'adequate' or 'good'.
- **National HSE Youth Homeless Group:** A national, HSE-led Youth Homeless Group was established in 2011 and includes representation from direct providers of youth homeless services in the HSE, non-governmental organisations, Irish Youth Justice Service and An Gardaí Síochána. Members of the group are collaborating on the development of policies and procedures, and their work has been perceived to be successful in enhancing coordination.
- **Proactivity, perseverance and flexibility:** Proactivity when need arises, perseverance and flexibility were identified as enablers of coordination of organisations. An example of proactivity is the leadership displayed by An Gardaí Síochána in hosting regional monthly meetings with homeless service providers in Dublin.
- **Shared understanding and common goals:** Findings from the consultation indicate that mutual respect, understanding and a focus on common goals help to overcome the potential for 'territorial thinking' between voluntary and statutory organisations.

Challenges

- **Lack of coordination:** According to the consultation, the agencies and sectors with which enhanced coordination is required are youth justice (*see Objective 4*), education (*see Objective 2*) and, for the transition stage, local authorities. The existence of different administration boundaries across agencies makes joint planning complex. Many respondents in the consultation reported that a common approach, continuity, prioritisation and vision are lacking. For example, local authorities placing homeless families can ban a child from being housed with the family due to anti-social behaviour; if they do not liaise with the HSE, the child is therefore actively made homeless. Even within the HSE itself, departments may not be connected and coordination is needed. This lack of connection has the potential to be exacerbated by the planned restructuring of the HSE.

  > 'We're all independent republics doing our own thing ... There's no joined-up thinking.' [Service provider]

- **Overly dependent on particular individuals:** It was remarked that effective interagency working can be heavily dependent on committed individuals within organisations and once these individuals leave their positions, collaboration may cease.
- **Organisational culture not conducive to interagency working:** Findings from the consultation indicate that organisations can be 'territorial', which impedes a more holistic approach to effective services. The need for communication, flexibility and awareness about respective roles was emphasized. Organisations need to be adaptable in order

to enjoy effective collaboration; stakeholders reported that information on roles and responsibilities is needed, in addition to transparency regarding the resources available to provide services.

> 'It's not re-inventing the wheel, it's not revolutionary thinking. It's going back to what it was before. Everyone became disjointed and protective about their service and maybe it's about becoming more fluid and flexible again.' [Service provider]

- **Need for better leadership and accountability:** Better leadership was reported to be needed at all levels in relation to addressing out-of-home children and the attendant problems that these children have. The need for greater flexibility and more joint approaches to care planning and service provision was a common observation.

Objective 10: Accessing services

Each health board will facilitate ease of access to its youth homelessness services through the development of multi-access information points.

REVIEW OF DOCUMENTATION

The *Monitoring Report* by the National Children's Office in 2003 showed little progress had been made in this area. In 2008, the Working Group drew on a 2005 report by the Education and Training and Advocacy Sub-Committee of the Youth Homelessness Strategy Monitoring Committee, which indicated that while there was a 'wealth of information on youth homelessness around the country … the information, however, is not easily accessed or understandable by young homeless people or those at risk of becoming homeless, being aimed primarily at service providers'.

Lack of progress in this area is probably connected to the lack of understanding in relation to advocacy, as seen under Objective 8 (*see above*), and it is not a coincidence that the 2008 Report of the Working Group also stressed the importance of advocacy services, particularly in terms of outreach to children with complex needs.

CONSULTATION FINDINGS

Facilitators of improvement

- **Community awareness:** Consultation responses indicated that effective dissemination about youth homelessness and services to practitioners, local youth services, accommodation/support providers, schools and health centres means that children who are homeless or at risk of homelessness can be more easily identified. Children can then be better supported if they seek help from members of the community. Good interagency working and structures to support it were reported to enhance community awareness.
- **Youth-friendly information sources:** While it was felt that homeless services should not be advertised, it was considered extremely important that children know where they can seek help and have access to youth-friendly information sources, such as the website www.SpunOut.ie, or advocacy services such as those provided by Empowering Young People in Care (EPIC).

Challenges

- **Better access to information for children and young people needed:** Children and young people reported great difficulty in accessing and navigating youth homelessness services. While the Youth Homelessness Strategy recommended a range of access points, findings from the consultation indicate that these have not been developed. This is likely to contribute to what stakeholders felt was 'hidden homelessness'. One young person reported sleeping in a lift while maintaining school life because he did not know where to turn for help. Some children found information on services by chance. Education programmes in schools on what children can do when they find themselves out-of-home were advised, in addition to the provision of a 24-hour telephone support service.

> 'When I became homeless … I hadn't a clue what to do … Somehow I came across Focus Ireland outreach number, that was the only point and this was after nearly two years of being homeless that I finally got a contact point.' [Young person]

- **More awareness of youth homelessness and youth at risk in communities needed:** A lack of awareness and understanding of youth homelessness and general issues relating to youth at risk was highlighted. Respondents considered that campaigns were needed to raise awareness and increase knowledge. In particular, it was felt that stereotypical images of homeless children need to be dispelled. It was suggested that information leaflets could be distributed in schools, hospitals, primary care centres and libraries. Training for staff working with children, such as in schools, was also deemed important. Children and young people reported not realising they needed help, and those they did turn to did not know how to help.

  > '[We] need to go back to linking in within community, youth clubs, local Gardaí. We're not doing that at the moment. We've become quite insular in some ways. If you make contact with us, well and good, but we haven't gone out there.'
  > [Service provider]

  Stakeholders suggested that the following information needs to be disseminated to local organisations and service providers:

  - directory or mapping of local and national accommodation and service providers, with details on availability and access;
  - details on the support services available and how they can provide support;
  - reasons for homelessness and advice on recommended responses, particularly out-of-hours;
  - appropriate programmes and supports available in relation to education and health.

Objective 11: Information systems

Effective information systems on homeless young people will be developed, including a database accessible to both voluntary and statutory service providers.

REVIEW OF DOCUMENTATION

The Youth Homelessness Strategy was founded in part on the recognition that there was inadequate data in relation to the problem, with the result that it was not possible to properly plan preventive and responsive services. The National Children's Office (2003) in its *Monitoring Report* stated:

> 'Four years after the Forum Report identified information deficits as a major obstacle to planning of youth homelessness services, several Health Boards still lack basic information systems and databases ... up to recently there were varying definitions of youth homelessness ... This situation should be improved by the introduction of a new statistical methodology on 1 January 2004. This system was devised by a sub-group of the Youth Homelessness Strategy Monitoring Committee and included a national standard definition of youth homelessness. It is anticipated that there will be more accurate statistics available in 2005 to assist planning to successfully implement the strategy.'

By 2008, the Working Group was still concerned that there was no single definition of 'youth homelessness' in use nationally, which would enable the levels of youth homelessness to be captured and tracked more accurately. The problem of definition – and the absence of a definition of 'youth' in the Youth Homelessness Strategy – is a significant problem and one that has been regularly highlighted in research undertaken in Ireland by Paula Mayock of the Children's Research Centre at Trinity College, Dublin (Mayock, and Mayock *et al* – see references):

> '... a Youth Homelessness Strategy was developed which, in effect, speaks only to the under-18s. The absence of an agreed definition also impacts on how data are and might be collected in the future. In the UK, youth homelessness is firmly understood to refer to 16-25 year-olds.'

This obviously has serious implications for the effective monitoring of services and the understanding of trends.

CONSULTATION FINDINGS

Facilitators of improvement

- **Structures to facilitate information-sharing:** Some consultation respondents felt that information-sharing had 'improved'. Children's Services Committees and other interagency initiatives were reported to have facilitated this and were deemed to be 'very beneficial'.

- **Using data to inform planning and development of services:** There were some conflicting messages from stakeholders on the use of data to inform services. The majority of survey respondents (78%) felt that the information was 'adequate' (39%) or 'good' (39%), but only 17% claimed that they had access to information on the number of young homeless people and only a minority of respondents (37%) 'usually' or 'always' used this information in the planning and development of services.

Challenges

- **Agreement on effective data monitoring needed:** The development of effective information systems was highlighted by many stakeholders as an area that needs significant improvement. It was felt that information systems are 'very poor' and 'not reliable', which has led to the misinterpretation of data. To facilitate the planning and monitoring of services, information on homelessness needs to be collected as part of a wider dataset on the health and well-being of vulnerable or at-risk children, to include data on categories such as gender, age, ethnicity, reasons for homelessness where that exists, interaction with services, and repeat homeless incidents. Service staff reported being unclear as to what data should be collected. This issue relates to the lack of clarity about the current definition of 'youth homelessness'. It was felt that the categories needed to be revisited and staff need training and support for data collection and interpretation. Effective data monitoring would result in ascertaining the full extent of youth homelessness, tracking children who have come into contact with services, identifying trends and examining the effectiveness of prevention strategies and emergency responses within a wider context of monitoring and evaluating interventions to support children at risk. It was considered that this would lead to more effective planning and service provision. Integration with the newly developed data management system for the adult homeless services (PASS) was suggested as a potential mechanism for data monitoring.

  > 'A huge part of our work is preventative ... That's the key to our work and the key to the Youth Homelessness Strategy ... What we are doing is avoiding them being one of those numbers, but nobody knows and nobody's counting the number of people we are working with to avoid that happening. That's the gap. They are capturing what can be seen rather than what can't be seen.' [Practitioner]

- **Information-sharing protocols need to be developed:** Findings from the consultation indicate that information-sharing protocols between services need to be agreed for appropriate exchange of information. Confidentiality concerns also need to be resolved. Respondents identified the type of information on a child accessing services that would be beneficial to share across services working with the particular child. The relevant information for case management included the reasons for homelessness and why the child is not in the care of the HSE.

- **Information-sharing between HSE Children and Family Services and Youth Probation needs attention:** Information-sharing between the HSE Children and Family Services and the Young Person's Probation Services was highlighted as needing particular attention. The integration of services appears to be urgently needed, according to the following comment:

  > 'Judges in sentencing young people to criminal detention generally do not establish who's the child's guardian and whether or not the child is in the care of the State (HSE).' [Practitioner]

Objective 12: Evaluation

Ongoing evaluation will be conducted at both local and national levels of the effectiveness of interventions to prevent homelessness occurring and of the services to assist and support young people who become homeless.

REVIEW OF DOCUMENTATION

There has been limited evaluation of the Youth Homelessness Strategy and what there has been is hampered by the absence of data (as outlined under Objective 11) and structural change/reform both in the health service and at Departmental level during the lifetime of the strategy. The National Children's Office carried out the first monitoring exercise in late 2002. This was in tabular form against the actions of the strategy, with returns requested from the Eastern Regional Health Area (ERHA) and non-ERHA Health Boards. The returns varied in detail. The table was updated in 2003, with the addition of site visits and interviews (NCO, 2003). Departmental files have no evidence of this approach being continued after 2003.

Under the 2001 strategy, the former Health Boards (now the Health Service Executive) were identified by the then Minister for Health as having the lead responsibility for implementation of the detailed action plan drawn up to address youth homelessness in line with the objectives set out in the strategy. In 2006, the HSE commissioned a *Review of the Implementation of the Youth Homelessness Strategy by the Health Service Executive* (Fitzpatrick Associates, 2006). This report was based on HSE area returns directly to the Department of Health and Children. The returns varied considerably in format, with some HSE areas reporting against the objectives of the strategy and others reporting against objectives they had generated within their own planning. The HSE 2008 Report of the Working Group drew on the earlier HSE 2006 report, subcommittee reports of the Youth Homelessness Strategy Monitoring Committee, recent research and the HSE's own collective knowledge and experience. Departmental files included a *Report of the Strategy Group on Homelessness Policy to the Cabinet Committee on Social Inclusion* in 2005, but there was no evidence of reporting to the Cabinet Committee on Children by the Minister for Children as envisioned in the actions under this Objective 12.

Monitoring and evaluation of the strategy over the last decade, like the planning approaches in Health Board areas, have been patchy and probably been undermined by a loss of focus due to health service reform, structural changes at Department/Government level, and an absence of useable datasets. The success in providing better services for children in care and aftercare, together with the diminishing demand for youth homeless services have also probably contributed to a loss of focus on monitoring and evaluation.

Although there is no systematic approach to gathering the views of services users, the 2012 report by the Ombudsman for Children, entitled *Homeless Truths: Children's Experiences of Homelessness in Ireland*, included interviews with young people who had known homelessness, providing a graphic representation of their experiences.

CONSULTATION FINDINGS

Facilitators of improvement

- **Policies and procedures being developed based on reviews of services:** Findings from the consultation indicate that the National HSE Youth Homeless Group is currently reviewing homeless services and developing policies and procedures on responses to youth homelessness on the basis of these reviews. The Group has recently completed a review of the use of Section 5 of the Child Care Act 1991 and has developed practice guidelines for its use. Further guidance and policies will be developed in due course, for example, on the use of supported lodgings. The Youth Homeless Forum will continue to meet quarterly. The Supported Lodgings Policy has been developed and implemented. The Youth Homeless Group will also continue to monitor the use of Section 5 and the numbers of children accessing emergency services due to homelessness. It also works closely with the Aftercare Steering Group.

- **Irish research:** Many stakeholders commended the research conducted to date on youth homelessness in Ireland and highlighted the need for more evaluation of the services providing responses.

Challenges

- **Needs analyses and service audit required:** Stakeholders said that an analysis of need and the capacity of services on a geographical basis would be helpful, and that this could be done at a local level with better interagency working. This analysis would also help identify gaps and obstacles in service provision and examine the appropriateness of the distribution of resources.
- **Research on best practice needed:** According to consultation findings, interventions and services are currently not being routinely evaluated and so that their effectiveness cannot be definitively established. Some respondents felt that only services with the best outcomes should continue to receive funding and that studies of successful practice in other countries could be explored. The challenge of assessing the effectiveness of preventive services was also highlighted.
- **More consultation with service users needed:** Findings from the consultation indicate the need to systematically include children in service monitoring and evaluation. Qualitative research on pathways into and out of homelessness is also important[4], in addition to examining the causes of placement breakdowns. It was highlighted that views and experiences should be regularly sought from children who are homeless, at risk of homelessness and homeless service users. As one young person who had experienced homelessness said: 'Our voices should be heard.'

[4] At the time of going to press, such a report has been produced by Mayock and Corr, entitled *Young People's Homeless and Housing Pathways: Key findings from a 6-year qualitative longitudinal study*, and is due for publication in 2013.

CHAPTER 4:
CONCLUSIONS

It is clear from this review that homelessness for children under 18 years of age is rarely an isolated need and that the pathways into homelessness are complex. Outcomes for children who are out-of-home have improved over the last decade. More children are dealt with by way of preventive services or, if out-of-home, by better care services. To ensure this trend of prevention or early exit from homelessness continues requires a holistic view of the lives of children.

There is no room for complacency and improvements are needed in providing children at risk with responses based on a comprehensive assessment of need and the provision of high-quality services and accommodation options to meet those needs. Key to improving outcomes for children is ensuring their transition to adult services is appropriate to their needs.

What is needed now is *not* another strategy for youth homelessness, but **for the problem of children being out-of-home or at risk of homelessness to be addressed as part of a wider, integrated and 'whole child' response to need.**

Overall, the Youth Homelessness Strategy was felt to have made a significant contribution to addressing the problem of 'youth homelessness', as defined in the strategy, and at the extreme end has helped ensure that children sleeping rough on the streets is a very rare occurrence. The proportion of children needing accommodation and other services solely due to homelessness has diminished substantially since the publication of the strategy in 2001.

The pathways into homelessness for a child often involve a number of different, but well understood factors. Work undertaken by Mayock and colleagues has provided good insights into why a child might become homeless and into identifying the facilitators and barriers to their exit from homelessness (see Mayock *et al*, 2006, 2007, 2008, 2011, 2012 and 2013).

Although the quantitative trend data are limited, there is current information about the low numbers of children presenting as homeless. Qualitative research also suggests significant successes in reducing the extent or minimising the duration of homelessness for children. There is no doubt that this has been facilitated by the dedication and skill shown by staff working with these vulnerable children in both the HSE and non-statutory sectors, which has facilitated many of them to be provided with preventive services, or maintained in care, or to exit homelessness and build satisfying and productive lives.

The considerable investment in services for children and families over the last decade, whether it be in relation to family support or alternative care, has contributed to improvements in the options available to these very vulnerable groups of children. There was widespread agreement among stakeholders during the course of this review that the strategy had successfully facilitated considerable improvements in services for children where there are child protection and welfare issues.

It is, however, the view of this Review Team that two implementation areas of the strategy were less successful. First, there was the need for a joined-up approach to assessment of risk for children who present as homeless, particularly mental health, addiction and disability services. Secondly, there was the need for improved linkages between State services at the transition from children to adult services.

4.1 Preventive measures

During the review process, services working with children who were homeless strongly emphasized the need to support investment in prevention, or at the very least to protect existing investments that support early intervention. Besides improving outcomes for children, the potential savings accrued from helping children stay in education, remain connected to their families, avoid the criminal justice system, have early diagnosis and appropriate treatment of mental health problems, and in preventing or intervening early in addiction problems, are all substantial.

Both international research and practice experience in Ireland emphasize the importance of family support in preventing homelessness or ensuring that where it does occur the duration is as brief as possible. Family support is particularly likely to be successful where it can occur early and where there is a menu of services available that can be matched with the needs of a particular child or family.

There is strong evidence to show that remaining in education is a protective factor in preventing youth homelessness and ensuring that children exit homelessness. There are a number of structural barriers to children and young people accessing education that are amenable to remedy, in terms of supporting children and young people to progress to third-level education. Supporting children who are at risk of homelessness in school or those who are not attending school is complex. Stakeholders said that the education sector should be a much more visible partner in developing responses to meeting the needs of children at risk of homelessness or those in emergency accommodation.

For young people leaving care at the age of 18 years, there is ongoing HSE financial support available to young people remaining in education and training courses. A young person who does not attend any educational or training course does not receive the HSE ongoing additional financial support; these young people are eligible for financial support from the Department of Social Protection. The option of re-engaging in education up to the age of 22, with a 3-year guaranteed financial aftercare support package, would greatly enhance young people's educational and future employment opportunities. It would also allow for greater flexibility and recognise varying levels of maturity and perceived need among those leaving care at the age of 18.

For young people between the ages of 18 and 20 who are homeless or living 'out of home' and have no formal care history, their paths to formal education can be tenuous. The Review Team found that there was some confusion among both young people and stakeholders in relation to what precisely young people in these situations were entitled to avail of, either in terms of social welfare or educational grants. What was clear, however, is that there was strong agreement that everything possible should be done to support continued educational engagement, as well as entry to higher education, for this vulnerable group.

Generally speaking, children and young people should be supported to remain in their communities where it is possible to do so and there are good examples of local community services that engage and support children. Stakeholders said that there needs to be better integration between local voluntary and statutory services. The continued development of Children's Services Committees across the country was thought by stakeholders to potentially be an excellent vehicle for this.

Research undertaken in Ireland and internationally demonstrates the very close link between being at risk of homelessness as a young adult and having been in the care of the State. There has been a great deal of work done over the last number of years by the HSE and its partners in the non-statutory sector in relation to aftercare. The HSE's operational National Aftercare Policy and the establishment of an interagency Aftercare Implementation Group are positive developments.

Stakeholders also said that providing effective services to this group of children is a challenge, particularly for those aged 16-18 who are recently known to the HSE, are vulnerable and at considerable risk of homelessness.

Stakeholders were also concerned about options available to support young people leaving criminal detention. It is important that this group is offered supportive services that are needed to help them manage the transition to an independent adulthood without becoming homeless. The support of this group should be monitored closely by the HSE Aftercare Implementation Group.

4.2 Responsive services

It is clear that the Youth Homelessness Strategy was put in place at a time (2001) when there were insufficient places for children who presented as homeless and where children were sleeping rough.

The availability and standard of services for children in need of care and support has improved over the past decade and this has impacted on the number of children accessing services through the homeless sector.

There has been a significant reduction in the demand for homeless services, which points to a downward trend in youth homelessness. The number of emergency placements for homeless children has been cut due to this reduction in demand.

There is, however, a strongly perceived need by stakeholders for more flexible services in city suburbs, small towns and rural areas. The need for an increase in emergency foster care placements, relative placements and supported lodgings for those over 16 was also highlighted. Since the beginning of this review, the HSE has increased flexibility in the Dublin area with supported lodgings for older adolescents and believes that there are now sufficient emergency foster care placements to meet demand.

Areas that have good interagency communication, managers with clearly identified responsibilities for alternative care and multi-agency fora for discussing accommodation and other needs of children – all reported being able to offer a more flexible and timely response. There was widespread agreement among stakeholders that Garda stations were not an appropriate place for children to routinely access out-of-hours services for the first time.

The HSE has stated that children who routinely access out-of-hours services in the greater Dublin region need not attend at Garda stations. Instead, they may go directly to the Reception Centre in Lefroy House. While many first-time users may access the service via a Garda station, if there is contact with the CIS during daytime hours, a risk assessment can be undertaken and the child may present directly to Lefroy House to access out-of-hours services.

Stakeholders felt there was a need for a more robust system for service planning for the accommodation needs of children out-of-home or those at risk of homelessness. This also reflects a need for better information systems generally in relation to assessing need and the outcomes achieved. The use of Section 5 of the Child Care Act 1991, to provide accommodation to children, was said to be inconsistent across the country. A review by the

HSE of its implementation has recently been undertaken and an operational policy has been developed. The HSE has decided that it is a suitable option, following an assessment, for those aged 16 and 17 years.

The provision of an individual comprehensive needs assessment was identified by stakeholders as a core factor in minimising the duration that a child would be accessing an emergency service due to being out-of-home. Stakeholders felt that where a comprehensive assessment occurs and a specialist service is identified as needed, there can still be difficulties accessing that service. Deficiencies were particularly highlighted for children with mental health problems and those with mild or moderate learning disabilities, particularly where they were not previously known to these services. The difficulty in accessing these services makes effective early intervention and prevention very problematic and places these children at risk of adult homelessness.

While the creation of the Child and Family Agency was generally strongly welcomed by stakeholders, some felt that there was a risk that with a more defined focus, it could potentially become more detached from services such as mental health or primary care, and so provide a less integrated service for children. It will be important for the new agency to actively prevent this happening.

A strong and almost universally held view by stakeholders was that planning and supports for young people between 16 years of age and the early 20s needed to be more effective and that the artificial division between child and adult services at 18 years of age led to disjointed working and poorer outcomes for young people.

4.3 Planning and administrative supports

Children and young people reported that it can be extremely difficult to access information about services. The HSE Children and Family Services has responsibility for the identification of child protection and welfare needs and the provision of services. A child at risk of homelessness has welfare needs and it is the responsibility of the HSE, or the services it funds, to provide such information.

Service providers reported that practitioners do not always have access to relevant information about services and supports, and some practitioners were critical of their own services in regard to this. Stakeholders felt that there is a need to raise general awareness of the problem of the welfare needs of children and to reduce the stigma many children feel when they are classified as being 'homeless' or 'in care'.

There was almost universal agreement among stakeholders that the collection, aggregation and analysis of information on children who are 'out-of-home' needs significant improvement if it is to be an effective tool in the planning and delivery of services. The lack of a robust information system over the years was a very considerable impediment to conducting this review. The recent development of counting child homeless as a subcategory of those accessing emergency services will be of assistance in the future. Monitoring these numbers, although currently small, is essential because they are liable to increase with any decrease in preventive and other services.

A more appropriate and useful definition, or definitions, of 'youth homelessness' is also necessary.

There was no formal plan put in place to evaluate the Youth Homelessness Strategy and the lack of good quality trend data would have made this very difficult, if not impossible. A robust evaluation process may have highlighted problems with the definitions and data issues generally, and enabled corrective action to be taken sooner. There is a need for a more systematic approach to consultation with children who are out-of-home. Although service users have been consulted by various agencies, this has not been done in a systematic way.

The strategy advocated the setting-up of local multi-agency Youth Homelessness fora. These were not established in all areas and, indeed, at the time of the review only one seemed to be operating as envisioned. While it is possible, or even likely, that other planning and management structures had overtaken the remit for these fora (or that the decrease in demand led to youth homeless coming off the management agenda), this was not documented or set out as part of a coherent and comprehensive response to meeting the needs of children in respect to homelessness.

CHAPTER 5:
RECOMMENDATIONS

This chapter outlines the recommendations emerging from this review of the Youth Homelessness Strategy. The recommendations are grouped under a number of themes in order to facilitate their implementation and provide a route map for the way forward.

All of these recommendations reflect a very significant desire from stakeholders to see:

- **A comprehensive and integrated multi-agency approach** to meeting the needs of vulnerable or at-risk children, which recognises the factors contributing to children and young people being out-of-home and at risk of homelessness, and addresses them with timely, effective and acceptable service responses.
- An emphasis on **prevention and early intervention**, which facilitates an early exit from homelessness where it does occur.
- **Flexible responses** in terms of accommodation and a flexible approach by services to meeting local needs.
- A **planned and coherent transition into productive adulthood** for children and a managed transition into adult services if required.
- That those young people over 18 years of age known to be particularly vulnerable to homelessness, because of having a history of being in residential or short-term foster care, receive **high-quality aftercare support**.
- **Information and decision support systems** that enable policy-makers, service planners and providers to monitor and evaluate activity, examine trends and adapt practice and policy accordingly.
- **A change of descriptor from 'homelessness' to 'out-of-home'**, which more accurately reflects the range of situations children may be in, so that in future we refer to children and young people as being out-of-home or at risk of being out-of-home.

5.1 Recommendations

1. Governance and supporting effective multi-agency working

1.1 The Department of Children and Youth Affairs (DCYA) should be the lead Department in relation to the implementation of these recommendations as part of a planned engagement with the Departments of Health; Environment, Community, and Local Government; Education and Skills; Justice and Equality; and Social Protection; as well as the Health Service Executive (HSE), HSE Children and Family Services and the voluntary and community sector.

1.2 The DCYA should monitor the implementation of these recommendations.

1.3 Emerging Children's Services Committees should be tasked with supporting integrated and comprehensive service responses at a local level. Where there are existing effective local interagency groups addressing youth homelessness, they should integrate with working groups for children at risk under the Children's Services Committees.

1.4 HSE Children and Family Services should ensure that there is planned and proactive engagement and linkage with relevant services outside of its own remit so that children receive integrated service responses and therefore achieve the best possible outcomes.

2. Emergency and follow-on accommodation review

2.1 The use of Garda stations at night by children accessing emergency accommodation for the first time should be stopped. HSE Children and Family Services should be tasked with developing alternative responses wherever practical.

2.2 HSE Children and Family Services should ensure that emergency residential accommodation in Dublin remains open to children throughout the day.

3. Meeting the needs of older adolescents

3.1 HSE Children and Family Services should plan prevention and early intervention services where they are required to support at-risk children in the 16-18 age group.

3.2 HSE Children and Family Services should continue to monitor the use of Section 5 of the Child Care Act 1991 as a way of providing support to children who are 16 and 17 years of age.

3.3 The DCYA should engage with other Government departments to ensure integrated services across key agencies in terms of service plan development and operational policy.

4. Continued support

4.1 As set out in the current National Aftercare Policy, the assessment for aftercare services and provision of services should apply to children who have been supported by HSE Children and Family Services under Section 5 of the Child Care Act 1991.

4.2 All children (under 18 years of age) who are discharged from a detention school or prison should have an assessment of their aftercare needs undertaken and, where appropriate, an aftercare plan should be agreed with HSE Children and Family Services.

5. Education

5.1 Children who are out-of-home and at risk of dropping out of, or being suspended from, school should be flagged for particular attention by HSE Children and Family Services and Educational Welfare systems. Every effort should be made to ensure that those who are in temporary accommodation are assisted in attending school.

5.2 The DCYA should engage with the HSE and the Department of Education and Skills to address any unintended barriers to participation in third-level education by young adults who are homeless or at risk of homelessness, particularly those who are looking to re-enter education.

6. Transition to adult services

6.1 The DCYA should identify service implementation issues with HSE Children and Family Services and engage with other Government departments with responsibility for mental health services, education, disability, addictions and accommodation in relation to children who are in aftercare and with those who are in need of ongoing support as guided by the assessment of need by HSE Children and Family Services in transitioning to adult services.

6.2 The DCYA, in developing the new National Children and Young People's Policy Framework, should engage with other relevant Government departments to ensure that youth homelessness and the specific needs of 16-23 year-olds are addressed.

7. Information and evaluation

7.1 HSE Children and Family Services should provide clear information about services for vulnerable and at-risk children through its website and other available information outlets. This information should include responses for practitioners and the voluntary and community sector about children at risk of being out-of-home.

7.2 The DCYA should decide on revised definitions for 'youth homelessness' in consultation with relevant statutory and voluntary agencies.

7.3 The DCYA should continue to support building and expanding the evidence base on successful responses to taking action on or preventing youth homelessness within an overall context of achieving good outcomes for children.

REFERENCES

Most documents are available on www.dcya.ie unless otherwise stated.

Commission to Inquire into Child Abuse (2009) *Report of the Commission to Inquire into Child Abuse, Volumes 1-5*. Available at: www.childabusecommission.ie

DCYA (2011) *Children First: National Guidance for the Protection and Welfare of Children* (2nd edition), Department of Children and Youth Affairs. Dublin: Government Publications.

DCYA (2012) *Report of the Task Force on the Child and Family Support Agency*, Department of Children and Youth Affairs. Dublin: Government Publications.

Department of Health and Children (2000) *National Children's Strategy: Our Children – Their Lives*. Dublin: Government Publications.

Department of Health and Children (2001a) *Youth Homelessness Strategy*. Dublin: Department of Health and Children.

Department of Health and Children (2001b) *National Standards for Children's Residential Centres*. Dublin: Government Publications.

Department of Health and Children (2004) *Guidelines on the Development of an Aftercare Policy*. Dublin: Department of Health and Children.

Department of the Environment and Local Government (2000) *Homelessness – An Integrated Strategy*. Dublin: Department of the Environment and Local Government.

Fitzpatrick Associates (2006) *Review of the Implementation of the Government's Integrated and Preventative Homeless Strategies* (sometimes referred to as the Smyth Report). Dublin: Government Publications. Available at: www.environ.ie/en/Publications/DevelopmentandHousing/Housing/FileDownLoad,1800,en.pdf

Fixsen, D.L. and Blase, K.A. (2009) *Implementation: The missing link between research and practice, NIRN Implementation Brief #1*. Chapel Hill, NC: University of North Carolina, FPG, NIRN.

Fixsen, D.L., Naoom, S.F., Blase, K.A., Freidman, R.M. and Wallace, F. (2005) *Implementation Research: A synthesis of the literature*. Tampa, FL: University of South Florida, Louise de la Parte Mental Health Institute, The National Implementation Research Network (FMHI Publication #231).

Forum on Youth Homelessness (2000) *Report on the Forum of Youth Homelessness*. Dublin: Forum on Youth Homelessness.

HIQA (2012) *National Standards for the Protection and Welfare of Children*. Dublin: Health Information and Quality Authority.

HSE (2006) *Model for the Delivery of Leaving Care and Aftercare Services in HSE North West Dublin, North Central Dublin and North Dublin*. Naas: Health Service Executive. Available at: www.lenus.ie/hse/bitstream/10147/51593/1/Aftercare_Services.pdf

HSE (2008) *Report of the National HSE Children and Family Services Working Group on Youth Homelessness*. Naas: Health Service Executive (unpublished).

HSE (2011a) *Leaving and Aftercare Services: National Policy and Procedure*. Naas: Health Service Executive.

HSE (2011b) *Review of Adequacy for HSE Children and Family Services 2011*. Naas: Health Service Executive. Available at: www.hse.ie/eng/services/Publications/services/Children/reviewofadequacy2011.pdf

HSE (2011c) *National Policy and Procedure on the Use of Section 5 of the Child Care Act, 1991*. Naas: Health Service Executive.

Lynott, M., Prendergast, C. and Dudley, D. (2000) *Report of the Review Group on Crisis Intervention Services for Children*. Dublin: Northern Area Health Board (unpublished report).

Mayock, P. and Carr, N. (2007) *Not Just Homelessness: A Study of 'Out of Home' Young People in Cork City*. Cork: Health Service Executive, South.

Mayock, P. and Corr, M.L. (2013) *Young People's Homeless and Housing Pathways: Key findings from a 6-year qualitative longitudinal study*, Department of Children and Youth Affairs. Dublin: Government Publications.

Mayock, P., Corr, M.L. and O'Sullivan, E. (2008) *Young People's Homeless Pathways*. Dublin: Homeless Agency.

Mayock, P., Corr, M.L. and O'Sullivan, E. (2011) 'Homeless young people, families and change: Family support as a facilitator to exiting homelessness', *Child & Family Social Work*, Vol. 16, pp. 391-401.

Mayock, P. and Sheridan, S. (2012) *Women's 'Journeys' to Homelessness: Key Findings from a Biographical Study of Homeless Women in Ireland*. Women and Homelessness in Ireland, Research Paper 1. Dublin: School of Social Work and Social Policy and Children's Research Centre, Trinity College Dublin.

Mayock, P. and Veki , K. (2006) *Understanding Youth Homelessness in Dublin City: Key findings from the First Phase of a Longitudinal Cohort Study*, Office of the Minister for Children. Dublin: Government Publications.

Munro, E. (2011) *The Munro Review of Child Protection: Final Report – A child-centred system*. London: Department for Education.

NCO (2000) *Report of the Public Consultation on the National Children's Strategy* (based on a report compiled by Colgan & Associates). Dublin: National Children's Office.

NCO (2003) *Youth Homelessness Strategy: Monitoring Report*. Dublin: National Children's Office (unpublished).

O'Flynn, J. and Chaloner, L. (2006) *Planning for Children – Improving access to services for children in private emergency accommodation in Dublin*. Dublin: Homeless Agency.

Ombudsman for Children (2012a) *Review Report: Follow-up on progress made in relation to the recommendations made on conclusion of the investigation into the implementation of 'Children First: National Guidelines for the Protection and Welfare of Children'*. Dublin: Ombudsman for Children's Office.

Ombudsman for Children (2012b) *Homeless Truths: Children's Experiences of Homelessness in Ireland*. Dublin: Ombudsman for Children's Office. Available at: www.oco.ie/assets/files/issues/HomelessTruths/HomelessTruthsWEB.pdf

Shannon, G. (2010) *Fourth Report of the Special Rapporteur on Child Protection – A Report Submitted to the Oireachtas*. Dublin: Government Publications.

Strategy Group on Homelessness Policy (2005) *Report of the Strategy Group on Homelessness Policy to the Cabinet Committee on Social Inclusion* (unpublished).

UN (1989) *Convention on the Rights of the Child*. Geneva: United Nations Office of the High Commissioner for Human Rights. Available at www.ohchr.org

Youth Homelessness Strategy Monitoring Committee (2004) *Guidelines on the Development of an Aftercare Policy*. Dublin: Department of Health and Children.

Youth Homelessness Strategy Monitoring Committee (2005) *Report of the Education and Training and Advocacy Sub-Committee of the Youth Homelessness Strategy Monitoring Committee* (unpublished).

APPENDICES

APPENDIX A: OBJECTIVES OF THE YOUTH HOMELESSNESS STRATEGY, 2001

Preventive measures

Objective 1: Family support and other preventive services will be developed on a multi-agency basis for children and young people at risk of becoming homeless. In particular, this will incorporate a generic out-of-hours crisis intervention service and where necessary multi-disciplinary teams to target at-risk young people.

Objective 2: Schools will actively support children at risk of homelessness, e.g. truanting children and those who leave school early, using the structures proposed under the Education Welfare Act 2000.

Objective 3: Local communities will be supported to assist children at risk of becoming homeless and their families.

Objective 4: Aftercare services for children leaving foster care and residential care, and other services provided by a health board, such as supported lodgings and for those leaving centres for young offenders, will be strengthened so that children are supported in making the transition to living independently or returning to their families.

Objective 5: Emergency responses will be provided promptly to children who become homeless; these services will be accessible and acceptable to this client group. Specialised 24-hour Reception Services will be provided in cities where appropriate.

Responsive services

Objective 6: A comprehensive assessment of children who become homeless will be carried out as the basis for individual action/care plans for case management/key working with the young person where necessary.

Objective 7: A range of accommodation arrangements will be provided for children who are unable to return home as part of an integrated response to the child's needs.

Objective 8: A range of supports will be provided to meet children's health, educational and recreational needs based on each child's action/care plan and aimed at reintegrating the child into his/her community as quickly as possible.

Planning and administrative supports

Objective 9: Health boards are responsible and will take the lead role in implementing the Youth Homelessness Strategy in their area; effective arrangements for coordination with both statutory and voluntary service providers will be put in place.

Objective 10: Each health board will facilitate ease of access to its youth homelessness services through the development of multi-access information points.

Objective 11: Effective information systems on homeless young people will be developed, including a database accessible to both voluntary and statutory service providers.

Objective 12: Ongoing evaluation will be conducted at both local and national levels of the effectiveness of interventions to prevent homelessness occurring and of the services to assist and support young people who become homeless.

APPENDIX B: ORGANISATIONS THAT PARTICIPATED IN THE REVIEW

Stakeholders from the following organisations participated in the interviews and online survey. The list of survey participants only includes those who voluntarily disclosed their organisation.

Interview participants

- An Gardaí Síochána
- Barnardos
- BeLonG To
- Children's Residential Centre, HSE
- Department of Children and Youth Affairs
- Department of the Environment, Community and Local Government
- Empowering People in Care (EPIC)
- Five Rivers
- Focus Ireland
- HSE Children and Family Services
- HSE Crisis Intervention Service
- Lefroy House
- Liberty Street Services, Cork
- St. Catherine's Foyer

Survey participants

- Aislinn Aftercare Service DML
- Ana Liffey Drug Project
- Ballyfermot Advance Project
- Ballyfermot Social Intervention Initiative
- Blakestown & Mountview Youth Initiative
- Blanchardstown Youth Service (Foróige)
- CARP
- CDVEC
- Children's Rights Alliance
- Children's Services Committees
- Co. Roscommon VEC
- Cottage Home Child and Family Services
- Co. Wicklow VEC
- Crosscare
- Dublin Institute of Technology
- Focus Ireland
- Foróige
- Health Information and Quality Authority (HIQA)
- Health Service Executive (HSE)
- HSE Community Services
- HSE Crisis Intervention Service
- HSE Social Work Department
- Insights Health and Social Research
- Irish Family Planning Association
- Laois County Council
- Le Cheile Youth Support Service
- Liberty Street House
- Liberty Street Services
- Limerick City Council
- Limerick Youth Service
- Longford Local Authority
- Meath Youth Federation
- Monastery Hostel, St. Vincent de Paul
- Mounttown Neighbourhood Youth and Family Project
- National Educational Welfare Board (NEWB)
- National Office Children and Family Services (HSE)
- Novas
- Pathways
- Probation Service (Young Person's Probation)
- Public Initiative for the Prevention of Suicide and Self-harm (PIPS)
- Rath na nÓg
- Sligo Local Authorities
- Smyly's Aftercare Service
- Society of St. Vincent de Paul
- South Dublin County Council
- Sportsreach
- St. Catherine's Dublin Foyer
- St. Martha's Hostel, St. Vincent de Paul
- Substance Misuse Service
- Talbot Centre
- Team for Separated Children Seeking Asylum
- University College, Dublin
- Wellsprings
- West Cork Development Partnership
- Wicklow County Council
- Youth Advocate Programmes Ireland
- Youth Health Service
- Youthreach

APPENDIX C: EUROPEAN TYPOLOGY OF HOMELESSNESS AND HOUSING EXCLUSION

This is the European Typology of Homelessness and Housing Exclusion (ETHOS), developed by FEANTSA in 2005 as a means of improving understanding and measurement of homelessness in Europe and to provide a common 'language' for transnational exchanges on homelessness.

Conceptual category		Operational category		Living situation		Generic definition
CONCEPTUAL CATEGORY	ROOFLESS	1	People living rough	1.1	Public space or external space	Living in the streets or public spaces, without a shelter that can be defined as living quarters
	ROOFLESS	2	People in emergency accommodation	2.1	Night shelter	People with no usual place of residence who make use of overnight shelter, low threshold shelter
	HOUSELESS	3	People in accommodation for the homeless	3.1	Homeless hostel	Where the period of stay is intended to be short term
				3.2	Temporary accommodation	
				3.3	Transitional supported accommodation	
	HOUSELESS	4	People in Women's Shelter	4.1	Women's shelter accommodation	Women accommodated due to experience of domestic violence and where the period of stay is intended to be short term
	HOUSELESS	5	People in accommodation for immigrants	5.1	Temporary accommodation/ reception centres	Immigrants in reception or short-term accommodation due to their immigrant status
				5.2	Migrant workers' accommodation	
	HOUSELESS	6	People due to be released from institutions	6.1	Penal institutions	No housing available prior to release
				6.2	Medical institutions*	Stay longer than needed due to lack of housing
				6.3	Children's institutions/ homes	No housing identified (e.g. by 18th birthday)
	HOUSELESS	7	People receiving longer-term support (due to homelessness)	7.1	Residential care for older homeless people	Long stay accommodation with care for formerly homeless people (normally more than one year)
				7.2	Supported accommodation for formerly homeless people	
	INSECURE	8	People living in insecure accommodation	8.1	Temporarily with family/ friends	Living in conventional housing, but not the usual or place of residence due to lack of housing
				8.2	No legal (sub)tenancy	Occupation of dwelling with no legal tenancy, illegal occupation of a dwelling
				8.3	Illegal occupation of land	Occupation of land with no legal rights
	INSECURE	9	People living under threat of eviction	9.1	Legal orders enforced (rented)	Where orders for eviction are operative
				9.2	Re-possession orders (owned)	Where mortgagee has legal order to re-possess
	INSECURE	10	People living under threat of violence	10.1	Police recorded incidents	Where police action is taken to ensure place of safety for victims of domestic violence

continued

		Operational category		Living situation		Generic definition
CONCEPTUAL CATEGORY	INADEQUATE	11	People living in temporary/ non-conventional structures	11.1	Mobile homes	Not intended as place of usual residence
				11.2	Non-conventional building	Makeshift shelter, shack or shanty
				11.3	Temporary structure	Semi-permanent structure hut or cabin
		12	People living in unfit housing	12.1	Occupied dwellings unfit for habitation	Defined as unfit for habitation by national legislation or building regulations
		13	People living in extreme over-crowding	13.1	Highest national norm of overcrowding	Defined as exceeding national density standard for floor-space or useable rooms
	Note: 'Short stay' is defined as normally less than one year. 'Long stay' is defined as more than one year. This definition is compatible with Census definitions as recommended by the UNECE/EUROSTAT report (2006).					

* Includes drug rehabilitation institutions, psychiatric hospitals, etc.

Source: http://www.feantsa.org/spip.php?article120

APPENDIX D: YOUTH HOMELESSNESS SURVEY (WEB-BASED)

INTRODUCTORY QUESTIONS

1.1 What type of organisation do you work for?

- Voluntary organisation working directly with homeless people
- Voluntary organisation working with young people
- Other voluntary organisation
- Local Authority
- Health Service Executive
- Local Development Company
- Probation and welfare service
- Gardaí
- Government department
- Researcher
- Other: ______________________________

1.2 What is your role in the organisation?

____

1.3 What is the name of your organisation? (optional)

____

1.4 What local government area do you work in? Dropdown menu (with 'not applicable' option)

OVERVIEW

2.1 Prior to receiving this survey, had you heard of the Youth Homelessness Strategy, 2001?

☐ Yes ☐ No ☐ Unsure

2.2 Since 2001, do you think youth homelessness has reduced or increased?

☐ Reduced a lot ☐ Reduced a little ☐ No change
☐ Increased a little ☐ Increased a lot ☐ Don't know

Please comment on what you think is (are) the reason(s) for this change or lack of change.

____

2.3 What do you think a youth homelessness strategy should address? (Please tick all that apply)

- ☐ Young people sleeping rough
- ☐ Young people in emergency accommodation
- ☐ Young people in short-term accommodation for the homeless
- ☐ Young people in families who are homeless
- ☐ Young people in women's shelter for domestic violence
- ☐ Young people in accommodation for immigrants
- ☐ Young people due to be released from penal institutions
- ☐ Young people due to be released from medical institutions
- ☐ Young people due to be released from State care
- ☐ Supported accommodation for formerly homeless young people
- ☐ Young people in insecure accommodation including temporarily living with family/friends
- ☐ Young people living in temporary / non-conventional structures, e.g. mobile homes
- ☐ Young people living in unfit housing
- ☐ Young people living in extreme over-crowding
- ☐ Other(s): ______________________________

PREVENTION

3.1 Please consider the following profiles of young people and identify the level of risk of homelessness associated with them.

	No risk	Low risk	Moderate risk	High risk	Very high risk	Don't know
Learning/intellectual disability	☐	☐	☐	☐	☐	☐
Physical disability	☐	☐	☐	☐	☐	☐
Alcohol and/or drug problems	☐	☐	☐	☐	☐	☐
Mental health problems	☐	☐	☐	☐	☐	☐
Behavioural problems	☐	☐	☐	☐	☐	☐
Lesbian/Gay/Bisexual young people	☐	☐	☐	☐	☐	☐
History of being in care	☐	☐	☐	☐	☐	☐
Experience of domestic violence	☐	☐	☐	☐	☐	☐
Child abuse (sexual; physical; emotional; neglect)	☐	☐	☐	☐	☐	☐
Separation/Divorce in family	☐	☐	☐	☐	☐	☐
Breakdown of family relationship	☐	☐	☐	☐	☐	☐
Travelling community	☐	☐	☐	☐	☐	☐
Other ethnic minorities	☐	☐	☐	☐	☐	☐
Discharged from health institution	☐	☐	☐	☐	☐	☐
Discharged from juvenile detention	☐	☐	☐	☐	☐	☐
Other: ________________	☐	☐	☐	☐	☐	☐

3.2 What measures are currently in place to prevent youth at risk from becoming homeless?

____

3.3 How effective do you think these measures are?

☐ Excellent ☐ Good ☐ Adequate ☐ Fair ☐ Poor ☐ Don't know

3.4 Since 2001, has the effectiveness of preventative measures improved or disimproved?

☐ Improved a lot ☐ Improved a little ☐ No change
☐ Disimproved a little ☐ Disimproved a lot ☐ Don't know

3.5 Are there comprehensive family support services in place to prevent young people from becoming homeless?

☐ Strongly agree ☐ Agree ☐ Neither agree nor disagree
☐ Disagree ☐ Strongly disagree ☐ Don't know

Please comment: ____

3.6 What are the main challenges to preventing youth homelessness?

____

3.7 What should be the priorities for prevention in the future?

____

RESPONSIVE SERVICES

4.1 What services are currently available to young homeless people in your area?

____

4.2 Please rate the adequacy of 1) Emergency Accommodation and 2) Move-on Accommodation Options for young people who become homeless in terms of quantity, quality, location, speed of access, and range.

	Poor	Fair	Adequate	Good	Excellent	Don't know
Emergency Accommodation						
Quantity	☐	☐	☐	☐	☐	☐
Quality	☐	☐	☐	☐	☐	☐
Location	☐	☐	☐	☐	☐	☐
Speed of access	☐	☐	☐	☐	☐	☐
Range of emergency accommodation	☐	☐	☐	☐	☐	☐
Move-on Accommodation Options						
Quantity	☐	☐	☐	☐	☐	☐
Quality	☐	☐	☐	☐	☐	☐
Location	☐	☐	☐	☐	☐	☐
Speed of access	☐	☐	☐	☐	☐	☐
Range of move-on accommodation	☐	☐	☐	☐	☐	☐

Please comment: ____

4.3 How often are *newly homeless young people* separated from those experiencing longer term homelessness?

☐ Never ☐ Rarely ☐ Sometimes ☐ Usually ☐ Always ☐ Don't know

4.4 How often are homeless young people housed within or close to their own communities?

☐ Never ☐ Rarely ☐ Sometimes ☐ Usually ☐ Always ☐ Don't know

4.5 Young people under 18 years of age attend Garda stations in the evening or night time to obtain access to accommodation. How well do you think this arrangement is working?

☐ Excellent ☐ Good ☐ Adequate ☐ Fair ☐ Poor ☐ Don't know

Please comment: ____

4.6 When young people are placed in emergency accommodation, how often are their needs and their family's needs comprehensively assessed?

☐ Never ☐ Rarely ☐ Sometimes ☐ Usually ☐ Always ☐ Don't know

4.7 How well do you think services are meeting the following needs of homeless young people?

Educational needs:

☐ Not at all ☐ Poorly ☐ Partially ☐ Well ☐ Fully ☐ Don't know

Health needs:

☐ Not at all ☐ Poorly ☐ Partially ☐ Well ☐ Fully ☐ Don't know

Recreational needs:

☐ Not at all ☐ Poorly ☐ Partially ☐ Well ☐ Fully ☐ Don't know

Please comment: ____

RESPONSIVE SERVICES (*continued*)

4.8 How well do you think services are meeting the needs of homeless young people with the following profiles?

	Not at all	Poorly	Partially	Well	Fully	Don't know
Learning/intellectual disability	☐	☐	☐	☐	☐	☐
Physical disability	☐	☐	☐	☐	☐	☐
Alcohol and/or drug problems	☐	☐	☐	☐	☐	☐
Mental health problems	☐	☐	☐	☐	☐	☐
Behavioural problems	☐	☐	☐	☐	☐	☐
Lesbian/Gay/Bisexual young people	☐	☐	☐	☐	☐	☐
History of being in care	☐	☐	☐	☐	☐	☐
Victims of domestic violence	☐	☐	☐	☐	☐	☐
Breakdown of family relationship	☐	☐	☐	☐	☐	☐
Travelling community	☐	☐	☐	☐	☐	☐
Other ethnic minorities	☐	☐	☐	☐	☐	☐
Discharged from health institution	☐	☐	☐	☐	☐	☐
Discharged from juvenile detention	☐	☐	☐	☐	☐	☐

Please comment:

____

____

____

4.9 Since 2001, has youth homelessness service provision improved or worsened?

☐ Improved a lot ☐ Improved a little ☐ No change

☐ Worsened a little ☐ Worsened a lot ☐ I do not know

4.10 What are the main challenges to providing services for and meeting the needs of young homeless?

____

____

____

4.11 What should be the priorities for service provision in the future?

____

____

____

PLANNING AND ADMINISTRATIVE SUPPORTS

5.1 How do young people access information on accommodation and support services?

____

____

5.2 How easy is it for young people to access information on services?

☐ Very easy ☐ Easy ☐ Moderately easy ☐ Difficult ☐ Very difficult ☐ Don't know

5.3 Do you have information on the number of young homeless people in your area?

☐ Yes ☐ No ☐ Partly ☐ Don't know

5.4 In your opinion, how adequate is the coordination of services and exchange of information between the Health Service Executive, other statutory agencies, and organisations working within the community and voluntary sector?

☐ Excellent ☐ Good ☐ Adequate ☐ Fair ☐ Poor ☐ Don't know

5.5 How could coordination between the relevant statutory and voluntary organisations be improved?

____

____

5.6 What would be needed to improve the planning arrangements and administrative supports which are intended to reduce the problem of youth homelessness?

____

____

CONCLUSION

6.1 Looking ahead, what do you think should be the top three priorities for action in relation to youth homelessness?

1. ____
2. ____
3. ____

6.2 Do you have any further comments?

____

____

____

THANK YOU!

NOTES